# The G~~~~
# Economists

# PEARSON

At Pearson, we believe in learning – all kinds of learning for all kinds of people. Whether it's at home, in the classroom or in the workplace, learning is the key to improving our life chances.

That's why we're working with leading authors to bring you the latest thinking and the best practices, so you can get better at the things that are important to you. You can learn on the page or on the move, and with content that's always crafted to help you understand quickly and apply what you've learned.

If you want to upgrade your personal skills or accelerate your career, become a more effective leader or more powerful communicator, discover new opportunities or simply find more inspiration, we can help you make progress in your work and life.

Pearson is the world's leading learning company. Our portfolio includes the Financial Times, Penguin, Dorling Kindersley and our educational business, Pearson International.

Every day our work helps learning flourish, and wherever learning flourishes, so do people.

To learn more please visit us at: **www.pearson.com/uk**

# The Great Economists

## Ten Economists Whose Thinking Changed the Way We Live

Phil Thornton

**PEARSON**

Harlow, England • London • New York • Boston • San Francisco • Toronto • Sydney
Auckland • Singapore • Hong Kong • Tokyo • Seoul • Taipei • New Delhi
Cape Town • São Paulo • Mexico City • Madrid • Amsterdam • Munich • Paris • Milan

**PEARSON EDUCATION LIMITED**

Edinburgh Gate
Harlow CM20 2JE
United Kingdom
Tel: +44 (0)1279 623623
Web: www.pearson.com/uk

First published 2014 (print and electronic)

Pearson Education is not responsible for the content of third-party internet sites.

ISBN: 978–1–292–00941–4 (print)
978–1–292–00943–8 (PDF)
978–1–292–00944–5 (ePub)
978–1–292–00942–1 (eText)

*British Library Cataloguing-in-Publication Data*
A catalogue record for the print edition is available from the British Library

*Library of Congress Cataloging-in-Publication Data*
Thornton, Phil (Business writer)
 The great economists : ten economists whose thinking changed the way we live /
Phil Thornton.
  pages cm
 Includes index.
 ISBN 978-1-292-00941-4 (pbk.)
 1. Economists--Biography. 2. Economics--History. I. Title.
 HB76.T48 2014
 330.092'2--dc23

                    2014007702

10 9 8 7 6 5 4 3 2 1
17 16 15 14 13

Cover design by Dan Mogford
Typeset in 10.5pt New Caledonia by 3
Print edition printed and bound in Great Britain by Henry Ling Ltd, at the Dorset Press, Dorchester, Dorset

NOTE THAT ANY PAGE CROSS REFERENCES REFER TO THE PRINT EDITION

# Contents

# Acknowledgements

I would like to thank my family, friends and professional colleagues who have helped and supported me in the writing of this book. I am indebted to the publishing team at Pearson and especially to Chris Cudmore for his advice during the planning of the book and for his corrections and suggestions during the writing process. Much of the book was written in the British Library building in King's Cross, London, which provides a wonderful, quiet atmosphere as well as a vast resource of knowledge and the kindly advice of its staff. Finally, special thanks go to my wife, Dr Kim Issroff, who provided a sounding board during the tough decisions over the selection of the ten economists, read the first drafts of the chapters and offered support during the whole process (as she did for the *Brilliant Economics* book published by Pearson Education in 2013).

# Publisher's acknowledgements

The publishers wish to thank The University of Chicago Press for their permission to reproduce Figure 7.1 from Friedman, M., 'Inflation and Unemployment', *The Journal of Political Economy*, 85, pp. 451–72 (University of Chicago Press, 1997).

In some instances we have been unable to trace the owners of copyright material, and we would appreciate any information that would enable us to do so.

# About the author

Phil Thornton has written about economics, finance and business for 20 years and spent almost a decade at *The Independent* newspaper as its economics correspondent. Since 2007 he has run Clarity Economics, a consultancy and freelance writing service he set up after going freelance. Clarity Economics (www.clarityeconomics.com) looks at all areas of business and economics including macroeconomics, world trade, financial markets, fiscal policy, and tax and regulation.

In 2010 he won the Feature Journalist of the Year in the WorkWorld Media Awards. In 2007 he won the title of Print Journalist of the Year in the same awards. In 2013 his book, *Brilliant Economics*, was published by Pearson Education. He lives in London with his wife and three sons.

# Introduction

'If I have seen a little further it is by standing on the shoulders of giants.'
*Sir Isaac Newton, British mathematician and physicist (1642–1727)*

All intellectual disciplines require great thinkers, writers, experimenters and cogitators who seem single-handedly to advance knowledge and understanding within their particular subject area. Of course the process of intellectual development is often a collaborative process. This can mean a number of individually brilliant people working together on a significant project, such as James Watson, Francis Crick, Maurice Wilkins and Rosalind Franklin who discovered the double helix structure of DNA. It may also signify the process whereby thinkers in one era build on their predecessors, as Newton acknowledged in the quotation at the top of this page. But ultimately it needs a big brain to move knowledge onto the next stage.

As with all professions and academic disciplines, economics has produced its own fair share of key thinkers whose work has stood the test of time and whose individual contributions are both recognised by the generation of leading economists and immortalised by popular folklore as being the giants on whose shoulders other have stood – and still stand. This book features just ten economists, although it would be possible to fill ten more volumes with equally redoubtable thinkers, including, for starters, the 74 economists who have won the Nobel Prize in Economic Sciences as of 2013. Given that the Nobel Foundation only started awarding the economics prize in 1969, even that only scratches the surface of the 250 years of the discipline's modern history.

This selection represents those whose influence has been most widely felt, not only within the economic profession but also in the way that governments, businesses, investors and ordinary folk as consumers and homebuyers make decisions. The theories of these economists can be felt in the way that governments design and frame their policies and policymakers justify their decisions. They also inform the thinking of business executives when making decisions on investments, pricing and marketing strategies. For the average person in the street, economic principles have laid the groundwork for almost every transaction they carry out and every decision they make, from the type of job that they do through to the school that they send their children to. More recently they have tried to explain why they behave in the way they do.

## Why these economists?

The ten chosen for this book are, relatively speaking, of modern times. Focusing on ten of the leading economic thinkers of the last two and a half centuries is the ideal way to illustrate this subject that is so central to our daily lives. The oldest, Adam Smith, was at his prime in the latter half of the 18th century while two are very much alive. It goes without saying that economics goes centuries if not millennia back in time. Economic thought has developed through the eyes of Greek, Indian and early European traditions with important contributions from philosophers such as Aristotle and Plato. Chinese economic thinking is also important, thanks to Confucianism, Taoism and the Legalists.

But what does 'great' mean here? The answer can roughly be phrased as those who contributed most to our understanding about how the economy works, either at the micro or the macro level. These may also be people who have influenced economics or come up with a new ideology, but that is a less important criterion.

Some of the economists in this book have lent their names to whole schools of thought or to particular economic theories that, since the onset of the global financial crisis in 2007–8, have become part of the public debate. Others, especially those whose talent was devoted to the microeconomics of how people and firms make decisions, are less famous but no less influential. In some people's opinion they are actually more important than their macroeconomics counterparts, whose reputation has suffered a dent in the wake of their collective inability to foresee the financial crisis.

One difficult decision was not to include economists who had created whole new disciplines such as happiness economics, environmental economics and development economics, to name just three. Around ten economists immediately come to mind under these categories. However, these are still seen as branches of mainstream economics rather than as new models for overall economic management. Critics might say that selecting the modern pioneer of behavioural economics contradicts that. However, in this case it seems that the move away from the assumption of the rational *homo economicus* and towards the idea of people making irrational decisions is increasingly looking to be a major structural shift in the way economists view the core tenets of their discipline. Hopefully this selection will start a debate. Feel free to make your suggestions by going to this link online https://twitter.com/GreatEconomics.

# Who is this book for?

In a word: anyone. In today's modern interconnected, globalised world economics affects every aspect of people's lives. This means that everyone now needs to be familiar with key economic concepts, whether they are a business owner, investor, employee or homeworker. This book seeks to broaden the understanding of the average interested person by seeing how the original thinkers developed the theories that are so commonplace nowadays.

This book also provides an entrée into the history of economic thought over the last 250 years. It picks up the move by Adam Smith to systematise the concepts of economics, a move that marked a dividing line between the era of political economy and the modern concept of economics. No history of economics would be complete without an understanding of the early – and different – contributions by David Ricardo, Karl Marx and Alfred Marshall.

What they had in common was a focus on the individual actors in an economy: individual consumers and businesses and how they made decisions. The Great Depression shifted the focus onto macroeconomics and the debate about how national and global economies operated in good times and bad and the role of policymakers. This debate, which dominated the second half of the 20th century, was dominated by John Maynard Keynes, Friedrich Hayek, Milton Friedman and Paul Samuelson. More recently the focus has been moved back to the individual by economists such as Gary Becker, with his classical approach to understanding why consumers and families make decisions, and Daniel Kahneman, a psychologist who laid the foundations for what is now known as behavioural economics. As we will see, some of Kahneman's ideas were heralded in the early writings of Adam Smith, thus bringing us round full circle.

Anyone who already has some understanding of economics will be enthralled by the range of backgrounds and experiences that led to the personal development and innovative thinking of our ten economists. But this book is also ideal for anyone seeking knowledge about economics for the first time. It takes the reader on a broadly chronological journey through the lives of the main figures of modern economics, which in effect tells the story of the development of the theory of economics over some 250 years. Readers can dip in and out: each chapter is a self-contained story about one original thinker and their impact on the development of economic thinking.

# CHAPTER 1

# Adam Smith – the 'founding father' of economics

'It is not from the benevolence of the butcher,
the brewer, or the baker that we expect our dinner,
but from their regard to their own interest.'
*Adam Smith*, An Inquiry into the Nature and Causes
of the Wealth of Nations, *Book 1, ch. 2*

Every Briton should know who Adam Smith is – or least what
he looks like. This is not because he is a celebrity or a national
treasure but because since 2007 his face has adorned the £20
banknote. Even without that *aide memoire* many people in the
UK and elsewhere in the English-speaking world have probably
heard others mention this long-dead economist whose name
and ideas still feature in news reports and politicians' speeches
more than 200 years after his death.

An explanation as to why people will know his name can be
found on the banknote. Underneath his portrait are the words
'The division of labour in pin manufacturing' followed by a
quotation in brackets: 'and the great increase in the quantity
of work that results'. This is taken from his major work, *An
Inquiry into the Nature and Causes of the Wealth of Nations*,
almost universally known by the shorter version, *The Wealth of
Nations*.

Although it did not garner as many sales in his lifetime as
Smith's other major work, *The Theory of Moral Sentiments*, it
is probably the first best-selling economics book. More importantly it was one of the first to attempt to convey the whole
of an economic theory, rather than one particular aspect or
treatise, in one book. It was more clearly written than other
contemporary accounts, which may have helped build its
success in Smith's time. But it also set out a way of thinking
that has grabbed people's attention, both then and now.

While *The Wealth of Nations* spans several chapters and includes a number of key theories that have stood the test of time, Smith's longevity probably comes down to a core concept that underlies his thinking; it is also what most people are thinking about when they quote Adam Smith in support of their argument. This idea is that leaving people to pursue their own self-interest will lead to the greatest benefit for the whole of society. As we will see, his theories were more complicated than that but there is no doubt that is the concept that has stuck.

# Early life and character

To say that Adam Smith was a precocious student would be an understatement. He entered the University of Glasgow at the age of 14 and three years later went from there to Oxford University via a scholarship. While he came from a comfortable background, his early life was tinged with sadness. His father, also called Adam Smith, a well-connected solicitor and comptroller of customs, had died five months before his son was born on 5 June 1723 in the small Scottish town of Kirkcaldy (the town's current MP is former Prime Minister and economics graduate, Gordon Brown).

Smith was brought up by his mother, Margaret Douglas, and educated by tutors paid for thanks to a specific legacy in his father's will. The posthumous investment paid off, as the fast-track university career showed. At Glasgow he came under the influences of some of the leading lights in the Scottish Enlightenment of the 18th century. Key among these was Francis Hutcheson, seen as the founder of the enlightenment movement, who held the chair of moral philosophy at Glasgow. Hutcheson's views on human nature and the role of the state in controlling behaviour appear to be highly formative on Smith's thinking.

Before moving on to his studies in Oxford, it is worth mentioning that Smith's life could have taken a very different turn due to a mysterious event that took place when he was aged three. According to several of the economist's biographers the infant Smith was snatched by so-called tinkers (gypsies or travellers, as they would be known today) and rescued either because of the intervention of an uncle or a change of heart by his kidnapper upon realising that a search party was after him. In any event, it may explain why Smith was mollycoddled by his mother through boyhood, during which he suffered from a range of ailments.

Smith went to Balliol College, Oxford in 1740, aged 17, on a scholarship known as a Snell Exhibition. However, he found the style of teaching and the curriculum much less appealing and challenging than had been the case in Glasgow. He later said that most of the professors at Oxford had given up the 'pretence of teaching', while the university itself was home to 'exploded systems and obsolete prejudices'. The dons at Balliol confiscated the copy of the sceptical work by his fellow Scottish philosopher David Hume, *Treatise on Human Nature*, which argued for the supremacy of logic over theology. Despite this, Smith studied for six years at Oxford and returned to Kirkcaldy reasonably confident of pursuing a career that would pay him a decent income. What it actually led to was a return to Glasgow University to teach logic – Smith never received or taught an economics course in his life – and the following year he was awarded the chair in moral philosophy that his teacher and inspiration Hutcheson had held.

Adam Smith was the Professor Branestawm of his day. Stories about his absent-minded behaviour abound. One has him escorting Charles Townshend, a former Chancellor of the Exchequer and a man who later plays a key role in Smith's economic writings, around a tanning factory, and, while discussing the merits of free trade, walking into a huge noxious tanning pit from which he needed help to escape. Another story tells of him putting bread and butter into a teapot, drinking the hideous brew, and declaring it to be the worst cup of tea he ever had. Finally, Smith went out walking and daydreaming in his nightgown and ended up 15 miles outside town before the sound of church bells in the middle of the night brought him back to reality.

Whatever sort of Scotsman he was, Adam Smith was no Sean Connery. While he was brilliant of mind, he was no paragon of beauty. One of the most used portraits of him shows a man with bulging eyes, prominent teeth, a large nose and a protruding lower lip. He is also said to have had a nervous twitch and a speech impediment. He said of himself: 'I am a beau in nothing but my books.' A French actress who met him in 1766 described him as 'ugly as the devil'. He never married and remained devoted to his mother, who died only six years before his own passing in 1790.

# A wealth of ideas

Before looking at the key theories in *The Wealth of Nations*, it is worth looking at his best-seller, *A Theory of Moral Sentiments*. In this book Smith the philosopher sets out how people make moral judgements. This is his rebuttal to the idea gaining ground at the time, thanks to the depressing vision set out by Thomas Hobbes in his book *Leviathan*, that humans are ultimately selfish and that the world would collapse into savagery without the controlling influence of the state.

In order to overcome this, Smith shows that the restraint on behaviour comes from the people themselves rather than from artificial control. He sets out the idea of 'sympathy' that people have for each other. While people might be selfish, they in fact 'render their happiness' to each other simply because they enjoy seeing the result. In modern-day terminology we would talk about the ability to put ourselves in someone else's shoes. Smith also set out the idea of an 'impartial observer' whom people have in mind when making a decision and whose approval they desire.

---

*Smith sets out the idea of 'sympathy' that*
*people have for each other.*

---

This is important both because it feeds into his thinking on economics in *The Wealth of Nations*, but also because it contradicts the popularly held view that the economics set out by Adam Smith are based entirely on a person's selfish self-interest and that people should care only about the costs and benefits of their decisions. As we can see, the original theory was more complex than that. *The Theory of Moral Sentiments* was published in 1759 and was immediately popular. It attracted students from across Europe to enrol at Glasgow to hear Smith lecture.

# From philosophy to economics

The book not only attracted a broad audience but also won Smith the financial backing of Charles Townshend, Smith's guest at the tanning factory. Townshend was the stepfather of the teenaged Duke of Buccleuch, and he persuaded Smith to resign his chair at Glasgow and become his tutor. The first 18 months of this role was spent in France, where Smith met and debated with the elite of French thinkers at the time, including Voltaire. On their return to London, Smith spent the following ten years writing the five-volume *The Wealth of Nations*, which was published in 1776.

One of the reasons for starting *The Great Economists* with Smith is that *The Wealth of Nations* laid out for the first time a comprehensive economic theory of the world. The full title gives a big clue: the book aims to establish how societies can become commercially successful. It is not an economics textbook: it is a manual of instruction to policymakers. The first volume looks at the productive powers of labour and how to distribute the results between different parts of society. The second looks at the accumulation of wealth and the third at how different countries grow at different speeds. The fourth volume criticises the agricultural and mercantile systems and the last one looks at how governments should raise revenue through taxation and what they should spend it on. Out of this long and detailed work there are perhaps six key concepts that have stood the test of time and for which Smith is best remembered and has had the greatest influence. We'll look at these key ideas now.

# The invisible hand

*Wealth of Nations* marshals the theories of self-interest first written about in *The Theory of Moral Sentiments* into a way of looking at how societies prosper. Smith aimed to overthrow the prevailing notion at the time, known as mercantilism. This stated that the only way to prosper was to hoard wealth, which

was seen as finite. Under this system countries should sell
goods to other states but put up tariffs to prevent others taking
their wealth.

Smith believed that real wealth was the sum of the annual
produce of the land and labour of the whole country and that
prosperity was based on increasing that. He focused on the
concept of 'natural liberty', the idea that people can deploy
their resources in competition with others. This process would
identify which activities were most worth doing. For example,
if mining produced higher returns than the average of other
activities then capital would naturally swing towards that area
and away from less productive areas.

Just as capital will head towards the industry that produces
the greatest value, so each worker aims for the job that will
make him or her the most money. In each case, as Smith put it,
this worker 'neither intends to promote the public interest, nor
knows how much he is promoting it. He intends only his own
gain, and he is in this led by an invisible hand to promote an
end which was no part of his intention.'

---

*Smith is laying out the basis for the
free-market mechanism of supply and
demand.*

---

Smith is in effect laying out the basis for the free-market
mechanism of supply and demand. Over time this will become
the general equilibrium theory, set out a century later and
formalised in greater detail by Paul Samuelson, whom we will
meet later (see Chapter 8), and other eminent economists.

Smith is not saying that people are motivated purely by self-interest, but that by following the path that benefits them most as individuals they also deliver a greater good for society. This is best shown by Smith's quotation at the start of the chapter – the idea that people have food for dinner every day as a result of the 'regard to their own interest' by the butcher, the brewer and the baker rather than because of their charity.

The implication is that society will be better served by allowing people to pursue their own instincts and desires rather than by allowing the state to intervene. 'I have never known much good done by those who affected to trade for the public good,' wrote Smith. 'It is an affectation, indeed, not very common among merchants, and very few words need be employed in dissuading them from it.' This is the long-term result of Smith's thinking about human behaviour in the *Theory of Moral Sentiments.*

But it also logically leads to the idea of a laissez-faire system of economic management, where the combination of all the millions of decisions made by people – shoppers, traders, bankers and workers – leads to a more efficient use of resources than if the government tried to manage the whole system. In Smith's words, everyone should be left free to 'pursue his own interest [in] his own way'. Any government trying to do this would be 'exposed to innumerable delusions' as no single wisdom or knowledge would be sufficient to outwit the collective weight of thousands of individual decisions. Instead Smith said the state had three duties: to oversee national defence; organise domestic security and policing; and invest in public infrastructure that would be otherwise uneconomic for private individuals to build.

# The evil of cartels

It is important to note how strongly Smith resisted one of the possible results of full free-market business practice – the growth of powerful corporations and monopolies. He was fearful of business people exploiting their power by working together to rig the market and keep prices high. 'People of the same trade seldom meet together, even for merriment and diversion, but the conversation ends in a conspiracy against the public, or in some diversion to raise prices,' Smith wrote. Smith was not an advocate of government intervention but believed that by allowing genuine free competition to rein, it would not be possible for businesses to form cartels as new companies would divert capital into that sector to undercut the cartel and drive prices down.

He had little time for governments that created monopolies, which, he said, kept the market under-supplied and thus meant that prices were pushed above the levels that people could reasonably pay out of their wages. 'The price of monopoly is upon every occasion the highest which can be got. The natural price, or the price of free competition, on the contrary, is the lowest which can be taken.'

He also warned that the monopoly of trade between Britain and its colonies distorted the allocation of capital and indeed had 'broken altogether that natural balance which would otherwise have taken place among all the different branches of British industry'. He also saw that slavery was not economically viable – an argument that would be used by William Wilberforce in his campaign for its abolition. In *The Wealth of Nations*, Smith said that work done by free men was cheaper in the end than the work performed by slaves, which was ultimately the most expensive. 'Whatever work [the slave] does, beyond what is sufficient to purchase his own mainte-nance, can be squeezed out of him by violence only, and not by any interest of his own.'

# Division of labour

This is the concept that opens the whole book and is therefore presumably the innovation that Smith saw as central to his vision of how economic growth was created. 'The greatest improvement in the productive powers of labour ... seem[s] to have been the effects of the division of labour,' Smith wrote.

What seems quite obvious now to anyone who has ever worked in an office or factory was seen as radical 250 years ago. Smith was writing amid the birth pangs of the Industrial Revolution that over time would see hundreds of thousands of people drawn into mass production factories. But even at this nascent stage Smith could see how better organised work led to greater output by each worker – what we would now called productivity. It is significant that his theory was based on the observation of actual economic activity rather than on ivory-tower supposition.

*Smith could see how better organised work led to greater output by each worker – what we would now called productivity.*

Smith takes us to a factory that makes pins. He realises that one untrained worker left to his own devices may manage to make one pin in a day or a handful at best. But by splitting the task into 18 different tasks shared between ten different workers – drawing out the wire, straightening it, cutting it, pointing it, grinding it, making the head and so on – they can produce more. But not just a couple more – Smith estimated that ten workers could produce 48,000 a day or 4,800 each.

But how do you achieve a 4,800 per cent increase in productivity? Smith identified three factors:

- Each worker becomes more skilled in his or her particular contribution over time compared with a jack-of-all-trades.

- Time is saved by workers not having to swap machines and equipment as they go through each individual task.

- This encourages the design of machines that make it easier to do the work.

In Smith's view this process contributed to the 'universal opulence, which extends itself to the lowest ranks of people'.

This explains why different people do different jobs. People migrate towards the jobs that are likely to pay them the most, which in turn will depend on how good they are at that job. Smith's analysis of what drives different rates of pay is particularly prescient given he was living in an economy based more on agriculture and raw commodities than on mechanised labour.

The five factors in Smith's eyes are:

- how agreeable or disagreeable the job is;

- whether it is easy to do or whether it requires difficult or costly training;

- how constant the work will be, i.e. whether it is full-time or only intermittent;

- the level of trust that the employer is putting on the worker;

- the likelihood that the worker will be successful in the job.

Smith used examples of his day, comparing the likes of journeyman tailors and blacksmiths. But through a modern lens his analysis still makes perfect sense. Oil rig workers are compensated for the arduous work carried out in inhospitable circumstances, compared with librarians, who tend to have quiet, comfortable lives (for the most part!). Lawyers and doctors attract higher pay than court clerks and medical orderlies, in part because of the years of extra training they have done. Consultants are likely to be getting a higher hourly pay rate than full-time staff, in part reflecting the irregularity of the work. Senior staff members will often get paid more, especially if employers are worried they might leave and take valuable information with them. Anyone who has been through a regular assessment process at work will know how pay rises can be linked to perceived success in the job.

## Free international trade

Smith did not stop with the division of labour within a factory. He could see it could be applied to the national economy. While making a pin might require 18 different people, building a ship – which will need pins as well as many other parts and skills – is a division of labour on a grand scale. As well as ship-builders, sail-makers and rope-makers, it will require a host of workers to produce the metal needed to equip the ship, from the tree-fellers to produce the timber needed to make charcoal, brick makers and layers to build the furnace to produce the ore, millwrights, forgers and smiths to turn out the metal parts and so on.

This analysis can then be applied between different countries, each of which can specialise in the activities in which they excel. Smith did not explicitly make that leap, although he realised a householder in England could have got his heat and light thanks to coal 'brought to him, perhaps, by a long sea and a long land-carriage'. It fell to his contemporary David Ricardo (see Chapter 2) to flesh out how countries could pursue a division of labour between each other.

What Smith did was explain why countries should specialise in doing what they are best at producing most cheaply. If a foreign country can supply us with a commodity more cheaply than we can make it, it would surely be better to buy it using the revenue created by our production of something we are more efficient in. Economists call this 'absolute advantage'.

Smith used the example of growing wine in Scotland, making the tendentious claim that it could be 'very good' – but only if you were to invest 30 times the capital needed to make the same bottle imported from France or another wine-growing country. He saw that attempts by governments to protect domestic industries by imposing tariffs on imports would be 'hurtful' because they would force households to buy more expensive goods than they could otherwise have bought.

# The market mechanism

What Smith saw was a giant system that resulted from these thousands of individual decisions producing a much more efficient result than if some central potentate attempted to organise the country's production. As he wrote: 'Without the assistance and co-operation of many thousands, the very meanest person in a civilized country could not be provided, even according to, what we very falsely imagine, the easy and simple manner in which he is commonly accommodated.'

At the heart of this is a price-setting mechanism based on supply and demand – although Smith did not put it in that way. He saw that prices of commodities – what we today might call goods and services – depended on the levels of the wages, profits and rents that were needed to produce them. The actual price at which a commodity was bought Smith called the 'market price'. The price is set by the relationship between the amount of the good brought to market – what we now call supply – and the demand by those with the money to buy it. When there is strong demand, competition between buyers pushes the market price up. Similarly, when too much comes on to the market at the same time then the market price will fall to the level at which the excess supply is sold.

The conclusion, familiar to economics students, is: 'When the quantity brought to market is just sufficient to supply the effectual demand, and no more, the market price naturally comes to be either exactly, or as nearly as can be judged of, the same with the natural price. The whole quantity upon hand can be disposed of for this price, and can not be disposed of for more.' Smith saw that commodity prices were 'continually gravitating' towards a 'central' price. In other words, the equilibrium price where supply meets demand.

Smith saw that it was free-market competition that allowed that process to happen. He warned that moves to regulate the market could lead to prices rising above their fair value. But left to its own devices – where there was what Smith called 'perfect liberty' – firms and workers would move their resources away from unprofitable activities towards ones where prices were higher.

# The role of government

If the government should not interfere in the operation of the free market, what should the role of the state be and how should it raise money? Smith devoted the longest chapter of *The Wealth of Nations* to this issue and many of his conclusions form the basis for debates over the public sector that continue to this day. Out of his detailed and complex thinking, there are some core principles that are worth setting out.

There is a clear distinction, in Smith's eye, between the functions that the state should carry out funded by general taxation and those that users should pay for. In the first group were the activities that were 'laid out for the general benefit of the whole of society'. These were the defence of the country against foreign invaders, and domestic security; and the administration of a system of justice that Smith saw as an essential ingredient in the efficient allocation of resources.

In the other group were institutions, or public works, that gave benefits to the whole of society that could be paid for by contributions by those who benefited from them. The spending should not fall on general taxation, with the burden being shared out according to people's ability to pay. To understand what he meant by that, you can look at those activities he believed should be paid for by the beneficiaries.

These broadly comprised public works and bodies that helped with business and commerce, and the provision of education. While Smith saw that, like defence or justice, they were too costly for an individual to pay for, he felt that the burden should be shared among those who benefited from them rather than taxpayers in general.

He highlighted good-quality roads, key bridge crossings, navigable canals and safe harbours as infrastructure whose requirements would be driven by the amount of commerce going through them. The strength of a bridge must be suited to the number and weight of the carriages which are likely to pass over it. This implied that it could be paid for by a small toll paid by those who used it. Not only that, but the toll should reflect the amount of goods they were carrying and thus the wear and tear they inflicted. While he acknowledged that society benefited from a well-educated workforce, there was no reason why the cost should not be defrayed altogether by those who received the immediate benefit of such education.

---

*Smith was happy that the burden of taxation should fall more on those with the broadest shoulders.*

---

This left open the question of how the state should raise the money to pay for those activities that were not paid for by those who benefited from them. As we have seen, Smith was happy that the burden of taxation should fall more on those with the broadest shoulders. He believed that taxes could be imposed on land, both on its value, what was produced on it and the rent it generated; on firms' profits, with room for 'extraordinary' taxes on certain activities; or on wages.

But Smith also set out four maxims of taxation – general principles that governments needed to follow when levying taxes on their citizens. They are broadly summarised as:

- *Equity*: the idea that people should pay tax in proportion to their income. He also believed that a tax should not fall predominantly on just one of the three main options of land, profits or wages.

- *Certainty*: taxes should not be imposed in an arbitrary way. Government should make clear how much tax people needed to pay and when and how they should pay it. Otherwise this would give too much power to tax collectors, encourage corruption and undermine taxpayers' trust in the system.

- *Convenience*: taxes should be levied in a way that fitted with taxpayers' lives. For example, Smith realised that it was easier for landlords to pay taxes on their rents if the bill came at around the time they received money from their tenants.

- *Economy*: the cost of running the tax system should be kept to a minimum so that the revenues were not wasted on administration and the level of taxes could be kept as low as possible.

# Long-term legacy

It is hard to over-estimate the impact that Adam Smith had on the development of economics. Much of what we today call microeconomics is derived from his writing, especially on the division of labour and the invisible hand as the most efficient way of allocating resources. All the economists in this book – and scores of others – have been influenced by Smith's writing whether they built on his findings, sought to expand on them, or tried to argue against them.

## *The resurrection of Adam Smith*

Smith's theories have influenced the modern political debate. He had gone out of fashion in the 20th century as the rise of communism showed the potential of the economic model set out by Karl Marx (Chapter 3), while the Great Depression of the 1930s encouraged policymakers to seize on the writings of John Maynard Keynes (Chapter 5), who argued for more government intervention to correct the failures of the market. However, by the 1980s communism was in retreat across Russia and Eastern Europe and the dominance of the state and the trade unions was seen as a brake on economic growth.

Enthusiasm for his theories received a second wind. Two politicians, Margaret Thatcher in the UK and Ronald Reagan in the US – and their advisers – seized on his ideas to justify rolling back the state and deregulating labour and financial markets. According to a popular urban myth, Thatcher was said to carry a copy of *The Wealth of Nations* in her famous handbag, and in her own book, *Statecraft*, she described Adam Smith's invisible hand as a 'bracing blast of freedom itself'.

According to Bruce Chapman, one of Reagan's Deputy Assistants in the White House, Smith was a hero to Reagan since he studied classical economics at college. Speaking at a memorial service for Reagan, Chapman also recalled that ties with little Adam Smith busts on them 'festooned every male conservative chest in Washington. You had a wide range of choices: there were green Adam Smith neckties, maroon Adam Smith neckties, red, white and blue Adam Smith neckties. If Ronald Reagan had been allowed to run for a third term I imagine there would have been Adam Smith hats and Adam Smith raincoats.'[1]

The interpretation by some modern writers that Smith in his famous phrase about the butchers and bakers was saying that self-interest – or even greed – alone was a sufficient guide to human economic actions has caused a furious debate. Smith did indeed say that people who followed their own self-interest would collectively benefit society as a whole. However, this is not the same as saying only self-interested behaviour is necessary. Smith approved of charity but did not believe it alone could provide solutions to problems of want and hunger. What he wrote on sympathy in *The Theory of Moral Sentiments* showed that he believed people were driven by care for others.

### From pins to cars

Even keeping away from the argy-bargy of politics, it is clear that Smith has affected the way many of us live our lives on a daily basis, whether as consumers or traders. Division of labour explains why workers on a car production line each add some

---

1. http://www.discovery.org/a/2073

part to the basic chassis, why busy bankers do not answer the phone themselves but have PAs, and even why we buy pork chops at the shop rather than reliving the BBC sitcom *The Good Life* and rearing our own pigs.

For businesses, division of labour has been central to production systems since the Ford Model-T car became the first automobile to be mass produced on moving assembly lines using pre-manufactured parts. More recently this has led to the growth in outsourcing, which both magnifies the specialisation of the job of making individual parts and also exploits different countries' absolute advantage in what they do. Toyota says that a single car has about 30,000 parts, counting every part down to the smallest screws. While some of these parts are made at Toyota, it has a range of suppliers that make many of them.

## No game of monopoly

All developed economies now have laws and regulators that aim to prevent the creation of cartels or monopolies, an ambition that Smith would have lauded. Privatisation programmes in countries such as the UK saw whole industries, such as energy generation, public utilities and the rail and aerospace industries, move from state-owned monopolies to privately owned businesses that, to a greater or lesser extent, compete against each other. However, what Smith would have made of the alphabet soup of UK regulators needed to keep them in line, such as Ofcom, Ofwat, Ofgem, and ORR (for rail), is open to debate.

Within the private sector, governments have acted to break up companies that have gained a monopoly grip of the market, such as the Standard Oil Company of New Jersey in the 1910s and AT&T in the 1970s. Companies that seek to expand by buying up their rivals usually need approval from a regulator tasked with preventing the growth of future monopolies. It is fair to say that the word 'cartel' now has only a pejorative sense – especially when applied to the group of oil exporting countries known as OPEC! All of these trends can be seen as stemming from Smith.

## Open global markets

The expansion of free trade has undoubtedly exceeded Adam Smith's wildest dreams. Referring to 18th-century Britain, he said the idea that freedom of trade would ever be dominant was 'as absurd as to expect that an Oceana or Utopia should ever be established in it'. Britons can now buy clothes made in South-East Asia, wine from every part of the world, and computers made in whole or part in the Far East. Businesses, as we saw earlier, can source raw materials and parts from countries that can produce them more cheaply than they could at home and sell to consumers across the world. Pharmaceuticals, software, aerospace parts and luxury goods made in the UK are bought across the world.

---

*The expansion of free trade has undoubtedly exceeded Adam Smith's wildest dreams.*

---

Decades of negotiation between countries to open up trade routes and establish systems to ensure free trade that led to the creation of the World Trade Organization can be traced back to Smith. But it was in the 1930s that the original battle between mercantilism and free-market trade, which inspired *The Wealth of Nations*, was put to the test. In the wake of the Wall Street Crash of 1929 and subsequent economic slump, countries put up trade barriers to protect their domestic industries. This prompted others to retaliate until international trade collapsed and a sharp recession turned into a depression. When depression threatened again in 2009, politicians stood together to reject protectionism.

And Smith himself? His personal legacy was to see his book sell out within six months, according to his 19th-century biographer, John Rae. By the time he died in 1790 he would have heard his work cited by the leader of the Whig Party, Charles James Fox, seen Prime Minister Lord North introduce new taxes based on his ideas and read the editorial in *The Times* newspaper of 3 August 1787 that *The Wealth of Nations* should be 'perused by every man who makes trade his pursuit'.

Ironically perhaps, given his strong views on the benefits of free trade, Smith ended his days as a Scottish Commissioner of Customs and the Salt Duties, a role he took up a year after his book was published. Rae says that the appointment was 'express recognition' by Lord North of Smith's contribution. While his supporters would say that his work did indeed lead to a greater wealth for nations, it is safe to say that on an annual income of £900 a year (£115,000 in today's values) Smith himself ended his days a wealthy man.

# Verdict: credits and debits

Adam Smith was clearly one of the most brilliant minds of his generation, but the question is whether his ideas resonate as clearly in modern ears. Certainly the core concepts he set out regarding the division of labour and the invisible hand and the idea that economic wealth is generated by trade and activity rather than by hoarding money are so embedded in western economic systems that it is easy to forget they originated with Smith. His contempt for monopolies is similarly well entrenched in today's business environment.

However, it is clear that an economy that embraced all of Smith's tenets without dilution would look very different from the UK or any other European country. While accepting the principle of the free market, many people are keen that governments intervene to check the invisible hand. The use of taxes and regulations to alter the way that markets operate in areas such as domestic energy supply, air and rail travel, polluting industries and housing finances show how far we have moved from Smith.

He is not uniformly admired. Because his thinking became so influential among right-leaning advocates of free markets it has been opposed by people at other points in the political spectrum. This hostility has increased since the global financial crisis of 2007–10 and the subsequent world recession, as some have found it easy to blame Smith's free-market doctrines for contributing to the crash.

For much of the last century up to the present day, governments have played a much larger role than Smith believed they should do. There is little mainstream support for the idea that the state should focus only on supporting the legal system and funding a domestic police and national defence system. With 40 per cent of the UK economy taken by the state in the form of social security benefits, the National Health Service and the education system among others, it is clear we have moved a long way from *The Wealth of Nations*.

# What you should take away

Adam Smith is justifiably known as the father of economics and his reputation will last long after he has disappeared from British banknotes. *The Wealth of Nations* has become the template for all the major textbooks that have followed it up to the present day.

His key ideas, which influence modern thinking within economics and business, include:

- Real wealth is the sum of the annual produce of the land and labour of the whole country rather than the monetary wealth it hoards. Open markets for trade are thus a route to growth.

- It is the 'invisible hand' comprised of individuals' self-interested choices that leads to the best economic outcomes rather than central planning.

- Division of labour, the allocation of tasks to individuals or organisations according to their skills or equipment, leads to the highest level of output – an idea put into practice by today's businesses.

- The idea of a 'market price' set the stage for the demand and supply graphs that are the heart of microeconomics.

- Left to their own devices business owners will form cartels that will raise prices.

- Tax systems should be fair, certain, convenient and efficient.

- The government should use tax revenues to fund the good functioning of the economy but users of infrastructure such as roads should contribute to the cost.

- Monopolies should not be allowed to develop as they lead to higher prices.

# Further reading

Eamonn Butler, *Adam Smith*, Institute of Economic Affairs (2007).

Ian Simpson Ross, *The Life of Adam Smith* (Oxford University Press, 2010).

Adam Smith, *An Inquiry into the Nature and Causes of the Wealth of Nations* (1776).

# CHAPTER 2

# David Ricardo – from immigrant to gentleman

'I am told that I adopt new and unusual language, not
reconcilable with the true principles of the science. To me it
appears that the unusual and, indeed, inconsistent language is
that used by my opponents.'
*David Ricardo,* Principles of Political Economy and Taxation,
*ch. 1, §1, p. 11*

# Early life and influences

Economists have a reputation for being dull folk who speak in
jargon. Imagine instead someone whose personal life contained
enough twists and turns to satisfy a Hollywood scriptwriter and
you begin to get a picture of David Ricardo. He was born in
1772 – four years before Adam Smith's *The Wealth of Nations*
was published – into an immigrant Jewish family in London's
East End as the third of 17 children. His first home was 36
Broad Street Buildings, near to the current Liverpool Street
station. In a fitting coincidence, the site is at the south-east
corner of the current UBS Investment Bank building at 100
Liverpool Street on the edge of the old Jewish East End.

Fortunately, given the harsh living conditions of the time,
his father Abraham was a successful stockbroker who had
chosen to settle in Britain after leaving Amsterdam. In time he
was appointed to one of the 12 brokerships reserved for Jews
in the City of London, known as the 'Jew Brokers'. Abraham
Ricardo senior started to employ his son on the London Stock
Exchange at the age of 14. By the time he was 21 in 1793 David
had branched out and opened accounts in his own name.

Then comes a twist. In the same year that Ricardo began to
gain commercial independence, he showed his individualism in

a more defiant way. He married Priscilla Anne Wilkinson, the daughter of an eminent surgeon in the City and a Quaker. By marrying out of the Jewish faith he had turned his face against his parents, who disowned and disinherited him. The exact turn of events is unclear even from a memoir written by one of his brothers.

However, it seems that the friends he had made on the floor of the Stock Exchange rallied round and provided him with the financial support he needed to continue trading in his own name and ultimately, it appears, outperforming his father. Just as the modern-day Hollywood film about financial trading, *Wall Street*, turns on a reconciliation between father and son, so does ours. While he never spoke to his mother again, shortly after her death it seems that Abraham made a token bequest in his will of February 1802 to his son David of £50 'as he is well established and does not need more' (the other 15 surviving children each received £3,000). The reconciliation was carried a stage further in 1807, when by a codicil to his will he added David as one of his executors.

But the swashbuckling action does not end there. By the time David had reached his early forties he had made enough money to start thinking about quitting the stock market. He began reinvesting his wealth in a string of country estates, many of them far to the west of London in Gloucestershire and Herefordshire. Indeed, one of his first acquisitions was the purchase in 1814 of the Manor of Minchinhampton in Gloucestershire, which included a large estate of 6,000 acres and the residence of Gatcombe Park, now better known as the home of HRH Princess Anne.

The following year he made one of his famous invest-ments, buying some of the £36 million (£2.7 billion now) of government war bonds issued just four days before the Battle of Waterloo. The premium on the bonds was just 2.5–3.25 per cent because of concern over the uncertain outcome of the war against Napoleon. After news of the victory arrived in London the premium soared as high as 16.5 per cent before settling at 13 per cent for the remainder of the loan.[1] In 1819 Ricardo took a seat in the House of Commons as MP for Portarlington, a 'rotten borough' – a voting district with a tiny population that was small enough for voters to be bribed personally – in Ireland. He used his position to argue for his economic beliefs to be put into practice and held the seat until his premature death in 1823 at the relatively young age of 51 with an estimated wealth of £45 million in current money.

# From finance to economics

But Ricardo is not as famous now for these dramatic events as he is for the economic theories on value, rent, trade and government debt that he set out in three books that he wrote. The story of the awakening of his interest in economics tells that he came across a copy of *The Wealth of Nations* on a visit to Bath in 1799 while his wife was ill. He later described himself as a 'great admirer' of Adam Smith and it is clear the work had a great influence on him.

He immersed himself in the economic intelligentsia of the time, counting James Mill, father of John Stuart Mill, as a friend. Mill senior was a key influence behind Ricardo's

---

1. *The Works and Correspondence of David Ricardo*, ed. Piero Sraffa with the collaboration of M.H. Dobb (Indianapolis: Liberty Fund, 2005).

decision to put his economic thoughts down in a book. He was in regular debate with Thomas Robert Malthus, the economist most famous for his theories on population and with whom he had major intellectual disagreements. He was mentored by Jeremy Bentham, the founder of the utilitarian philosophy. He became a fully paid-up member of London intellectual society, being a member of a number of leading clubs.

# An economic theory

Unlike Smith, Ricardo did not publish an all-encompassing theory of how an economy operates but focused on the core areas where he felt he could make a contribution, building on – and sometimes overturning – theories set out by Smith, Malthus and others. *Principles of Political Economy and Taxation* was his second book, published in 1817, and its 33 chapters cover a range of issues that Ricardo saw as central to understanding an economic system. Not all have stood the test of time. He is now most famous for his theories on international trade and on the impact of government spending, both of which are argued over to this day, and for his scientific arguments against erecting tariffs on imports.

---

*Ricardo did not publish an all-encompassing theory of how an economy operates but focused on core areas.*

---

But before getting on to those it is worth looking at what Ricardo said about the general workings of the economy, as this influenced many economists who followed him. Ricardo wanted to explain how the results of industry were shared between landowners, workers and 'capitalists' and how that affected rents, wages and profits respectively. In other words, he focused on how wealth was distributed as much as how it was created.

He built a model of the economy based on agriculture, and in particular the staple crop of corn, which was still predominant at the time. He saw that with a rising population, demand for food would increase and, to meet that, farmers would have to bring less fertile land into use. The return on that land would not be as great as before. Indeed, as more and more land was brought into use, the extra profit coming from each new strip would fall, an idea economists now call the law of diminishing returns. At some point there would be no point cultivating any further land, as there would be no reward from cultivating it.

Ricardo defined farmers as capitalist tenant farmers who paid rent to landlords and made profits. As these farmers tilled less fertile land they needed to invest more capital, so pushing costs up. As food prices rose, workers' wages would have to go up – assuming that they needed to eat to live and work. Landlords would demand more rent for the more profitable land and ultimately this meant that profits fell for entrepreneurs. In other words, as capital built up rents would rise but profits would fall. For doctrinal experts, this contradicted Smith's assertion that higher wages lead to higher profits and lower rents. As Ricardo himself put it in *On the Principles of Political Economy and Taxation*: 'There can be no rise in the value of labour without a fall of profits. If the corn is to be divided between the farmer and the labourer, the larger the proportion that is given to the latter, the less will remain for the former.'

One implication that Ricardo drew out was that as wages rose, goods that were produced in a capital-intensive way became cheaper relative to those that were labour intensive, leading to greater demand for the former. Similarly, if wages fall then firms substitute labour for machinery. This pattern – known now as the Ricardo effect – was based on Smith's idea that capitalists would pursue the most efficient course of action for their own profit, thus leading to the best outcome for society.

Sadly, Ricardo believed that at some point the situation would become terminal. As farmers exhausted the lands, field by field, and the population grew, eventually starvation would set in as it became impossible to produce enough food to feed the workers at any price. Ricardo called this the 'stationary state' and it is based on the theories set out by Malthus. Malthus, who was a cleric as well as a scholar, said that starvation would result as projected population growth exceeded the rate of increase in the food supply. For this he was branded dismal by fellow philosopher Thomas Carlyle, who went on to condemn the whole of economics as the 'dismal science'.

# He fought the Corn Laws … and the law won

The reason for focusing on this aspect of Ricardo's thinking – and not his take on value or his section on currency and banks among many others – is that it formed the intellectual basis for his attack on the Corn Laws, a piece of legislation that had a similar impact on the political debate as the Poll Tax did on Britain 200 years later.

During the Napoleonic wars – the end of which led to
Ricardo's fortune – there was a sharp rise in the price of corn
and in the rents earned by landlords. In 1813 MPs called for
foreign corn imports to be banned until the price of domestic
corn hit £4 per quarter – a unit roughly equal to 220kg. When
peace broke out in 1815, corn prices collapsed and the Corn
Law was imposed in order to defend the domestic farm sector,
and by implication the rural landowners. As Ricardo said in his
article on the issue, *An Essay on the Influence of a Low Price
of Corn on the Profits of Stock*, 'the interest of the landlord
is always opposed to the interest of every other class in the
community'.

Ricardo argued that these trade barriers kept food prices
artificially high and encouraged an excessive rent. He said that
it was wrong to argue that corn had cost more because landlords
kept rents too high. Rather, the prices had risen because of a
lack of imports during wartime and this encouraged entrepreneurs into the farming industry to get a share of these profits,
just as he argued in his writings. 'The sole effect of high duties
on the importation either of manufactures or of corn … is to
divert a portion of capital to an employment, which it would not
naturally seek. It causes a pernicious distribution of the general
funds of the society – it bribes a manufacturer to commence or
continue in a comparatively less profitable employment.'

By creating a virtual monopoly for the supply of corn, the
government effectively pushed corn prices up, which in turn
led to a surge in the cost of staple foods such as bread for
workers in the fast-growing factories in cities. This ultimately
hit the profits of the new industrial bourgeoisie. Ricardo argued
vociferously in Parliament that it would be much better for
Britain to allow the import of cheap grain and use the capital
that would no longer be invested in growing corn to be diverted

towards activities, such as manufacturing, that it did better. Sadly the Corn Laws were not repealed until 1846, 23 years after Ricardo's death.

# Trading places – Ricardo's innovation

That story provides a useful segue to one of the two theories for which Ricardo is best remembered. We remember that Smith showed how a country should export to a partner the output of what it did best and use the money to buy in what it could not make as efficiently itself. But what if a country is worse in all products than another country – should it simply shut up shop, import everything and hope for a windfall?

> *Ricardo showed that it made sense for two countries to trade with each other even if one cannot produce anything better than its rival.*

Ricardo showed that it made sense for two countries to trade with each other even if one cannot produce anything better than its rival. Had the Nobel Prize been around in the early 1800s Ricardo would surely have scooped it. His theorem states that a country should concentrate on what it is better at compared with the alternatives. Ricardo used cloth and wine and Portugal and England, which even then was worse at making both. To make it easier to understand and more relevant to modern ears, let us assume that two countries, South Korea and Taiwan, produce two things and not much else – headphones and MP3 players.

It takes workers in Taiwan 120 person-hours to produce
1,000 headphones and 100 hours to make 1,000 MP3s (assume
they are worth broadly the same). If it takes South Korean
workers just 80 hours to make the same amount of headphones
and 90 hours for the MP3 players, then South Korea has an
absolute advantage in both. A non-economist should say South
Korea should carry on making both and not import either.
What Ricardo did was to turn this on its head and show that
the counter-intuitive idea – that South Korea should abandon
one of the two and import from Taiwan – not only made mathematical sense but would also lead to higher global economic
activity.

| Person-hours of work needed to make 1,000 units | | |
| --- | --- | --- |
| Country | Headphones | MP3s |
| Taiwan | 120 | 100 |
| South Korea | 80 | 90 |

Just by looking at the figures you can see that South Korea
may be more efficient at making both but is less efficient
at MP3s than it is at headphones. You can also see that the
productivity gap between the two countries is much smaller
for those devices than for headphones. By devoting all its
energy to making headphones South Korea will produce more
headphones in 1,000 hours than the total of headphones and
MP3 players. It will be more efficient for Taiwan to shift to
MP3s. By giving up what they are less good at they will produce
more of what they are better at. The box spells out the process
and shows how total output actually increases.

## 'The science bit'

If we assume that both countries spend 900 hours producing each good we can add up the total output (the number is chosen to make the maths simpler). In 900 hours Taiwan would produce 7,500 headphones (900 ÷ 120 = 7.5 lots of 1,000 units) and 9,000 MP3s (900 ÷ 90 = 10 lots). In the same time South Korea's factories turn out 11,250 headphones (900 ÷ 80 = 11.25 lots) and 10,000 MP3s (900 ÷ 90 = 10 lots). The total output is 37,750. If Korea shuts its MP3 factory and moves the workers on to headphones, in 2,000 hours it will produce 25,000 of the listening devices. Taiwan closes its headphone plant and focuses on MP3s, where its workers in 2,000 hours make 20,000 players. The total output is now 45,000 or a near-20 per cent increase.

The Nobel laureate Paul Samuelson, whom we shall meet later (in Chapter 8), was once challenged by the mathematician Stanislaw Ulam to 'name one proposition in all of the social sciences which is both true and non-trivial'. It was several years later that he thought of the correct response: comparative advantage. 'That it is logically true need not be argued before a mathematician; that it is not trivial is attested by the thousands of important and intelligent men who have never been able to grasp the doctrine for themselves or to believe it after it was explained to them.' In a 1972 article, *The Way of an Economist*, Samuelson refers to Ricardo's wine and cloth example as the 'four magic numbers'.

In terms of Ricardo's arguments in the House of Commons the message of this piece of writing is to say to politicians that Britain would be richer overall if it bought the corn and food that France could produce more efficiently and sell more cheaply than British farmers, who should focus their effort on doing what Britain did better – manufacturing.


## Borrow now, pay later: how taxpayers see government debt

The second main concept that still influences economics today also has a less-than-catchy name – Ricardian equivalence. It is the idea that governments that borrow money to fund a particular project will find that the economic impact is offset as taxpayers cut their spending to put money aside to cover the future tax bill they know is coming.

Not only does it have an odd name but it is not certain that Ricardo was totally convinced by the logic – even though it was he who first set out the idea. It took economists long after his death to flesh out the thinking and attach his name to it.

In 1820 the former stockbroker wrote an essay entitled *Essay on the Funding System*, in which he considers the best mode of providing for a country's annual expenditure both in war and peace (he was writing just five years after the Battle of Waterloo). Faced with the need to find £20 million a year to fight another war, the country would have to choose between three different ways of paying for it. These were:

- hiking taxes now to pay for the cost;

- borrowing the money every year and paying the interest;

- borrowing the money but also imposing a tax to effectively cover the interest payments (similar in a way to today's interest-only mortgage).

Ricardo argued that each strategy would have an economic impact. These would be:

- the equivalent to a £20 million tax rise up-front;

- £1 million per annum forever;

- £1.2 million a year for 45 years.

The implication is that people will realise that they will have to pay for the debt in the form of higher taxes whether now or in 45 years' time. On that basis Ricardo favoured the up-front tax, both because once the war was over then the tax could be cut back and also because it would make it easier for citizens to lobby against an unpopular war. He said that people would see the war as burdensome only in proportion to what they were at the moment called to pay for it in taxes without reflecting on the probable duration of such taxes.

Ricardo himself in his essay appears to play down that link, saying that it would be difficult to convince someone with a nest egg of £20,000 that a perpetual payment of £50 a year for 20 years was as burdensome as a single tax of £1,000. 'He would have some vague notion that the £50 per annum would be paid by posterity, and would not be paid by him.' But, as we shall see shortly, it was later economists who built on this idea to lay out the proposition that an increase in the public deficit is matched by increased savings by the private sector.

# Long-term legacy

You would have to search hard to find a politician citing David Ricardo in a major speech. But, unlike Smith, his influence lies in the specific ideas for which he is most famous rather than for one encyclopaedic vision of economics. That is not to diminish the impact of Ricardo's criticism of Smith's ideas, which helped develop the doctrine of classical economics, or of his own ideas that provided a platform for later economists to build on. One of those, as we shall see (in Chapter 3), was the communist Karl Marx. But it is Ricardo's ideas on free trade and on protectionism and government debate that carry echoes in today's political debates and news reports.

## *Global free trade*

At first glance there does not seem to be much in common between David Ricardo's Georgian England and today's modern homes that are bristling with technology and whose kitchen tables and bedroom cupboards are groaning with the weight of fruit and fashion articles from across the world. But the fact is that the current system of free trade owes a lot to Ricardo's thinking about England and Portugal and wine and cloth.

---

*The current system of free trade owes a lot to Ricardo's thinking.*

---

The idea that free trade benefits all countries and specifically that a rich country trading with a poor country makes both better off is at the heart of the World Trade Organization

(WTO) and its predecessor, the General Agreement on Tariffs and Trade (GATT). These international bodies were the result of negotiations between a large majority of the world's countries – there are now 159 WTO members – who were keen to open up their economies to world trade.

However, there are costs involved, just as Ricardo recognised when he recommended that Portugal 'employ her capital' in the production of wine rather than cloth. While in the long run Portugal would gain, it would cause short-term misery for the generation of clothmakers who would struggle to retrain as vintners.

The debate became live in the UK in the decade before the global financial crisis as the growing trend of 'offshoring' back-office jobs such as call centres and data entry personnel created fears that jobs were being lost to emerging markets such as India. Similarly in the United States, presidential candidate Ross Perot warned voters that signing up to the North American Free Trade Agreement would be marked by a 'giant sucking sound' of manufacturing jobs being lost to Mexico. The focus of government policy in response has been to help with retraining workers rather than to try to keep alive industries in which the country can no longer succeed.

## Corn and the Great Depression

The other side of the free-trade coin is protectionism, and the reason the WTO needs to exist is to ensure that countries play by the 'rules' of fair trade. The last few decades have seen claim and counter-claim over protectionist policies by governments to protect an array of industries including passenger planes, steel, solar panels, beef, prawns, cars, shoes and bananas.

Governments often find themselves under pressure for domestic industries to put up tariffs or more modern and sophisticated defences such as environmental and labour standards to protect their firms from what they see as unfair competition. Ricardo would have recognised the terms of the arguments over beef reared using genetically modified organisms as similar to those employed in a pre-technology era by rural landowners in 19th-century England.

Ricardo would have joined the ranks of 20th-century economists urging the major powers not to block imports in the wake of the recession brought on by the Wall Street Crash of 1929. The United States responded to the downturn by imposing the highest tariffs on record in an attempt to divert spending towards goods produced in the US rather than on imports. Seeing the threat to their own industries, other governments retaliated with tariffs, with the result that international trade fell by half. More than 1,000 economists signed a petition to the US government warning that the Smoot-Hawley Tariff Act would have disastrous economic repercussions.

Fast forward to 2009 when the world was seen as teetering on the brink of a new depression in the wake of the collapse of Lehman Brothers. This time world leaders took a leaf out of Ricardo's books and agreed not to embark on protectionist measures. As then British prime minister Gordon Brown said in the run-up to the London summit of the G20: 'Protectionism must be rejected as protectionism is the politics of defeatism, retreat and fear and in the end protects no one at all.'[2]

---

2. http://www.europarl.europa.eu/sides/getDoc.do?pubRef=-//EP//
   TEXT+IM-PRESS+20090323IPR52329+0+DOC+XML+V0//EN

## *Austerity or stimulus*

Ricardo's musings on the impact of government debt have received a new life over the last four decades and most specifically in the wake of the recent global financial crisis. In 2009, at the same time that leaders were taking Ricardo's advice on free trade, they were also working together to inject an estimated $1 trillion into the world economy to prevent what had been described as the 'Great Recession' developing into a depression. This inevitably involved governments taking on vast debts to be paid back by future taxpayers to get the 2009 economy back to life.

> *Ricardo's musings on the impact of government debt have received a new life over the last four decades.*

Ricardo's initial thoughts were used as a foundation by Harvard economist Robert Barro to form a fully fledged theory, now widely known as Barro-Ricardo equivalence – although he later admitted he was in 'blissful ignorance' of Ricardo at the time of writing his 1974 paper. The American economist said that if one assumed that families wanted to pass their wealth on to their children – what he called 'intergenerational altruism' – then they would take into account future taxes coming down the line to pay off the debt.

Since households are looking forward not just over their own life but over the lives of their children, they know that a debt-financed tax cut today implies an increase in future taxes that is equal – in present value – to the tax cut. Since the tax cut does not make consumers better off, they will not increase their spending but save the full tax cut in order to repay the future tax liability. Private saving therefore rises by the amount public saving falls, leaving national saving unchanged.

Critics of this theory, which many see as an intellectual justification for stopping government spending to help out an ailing economy, have sought to rebut both the assumptions and the implications. They say not all people take such a rational view and many will not look that far ahead and instead decide to pay off current debts or spend some of the extra money. A poll by Ipsos MORI in 1997 that looked at what people did with their windfalls from the wave of building society mutualisations found that almost half was spent and most of that on home improvements.[3]

While that relates to a private sector windfall, research into a one-off $1.17 billion payout by the Singaporean government, ranging from $78 to $702 to 2.5 million adults in February 2001, found that for each dollar received, consumers on average spent 90 cents, during the ten months after the announcement.[4] This debate will doubtless continue as economists try to work out the impacts of the stimulus measures in the wake of the global financial crisis.

---

3. http://www.ipsos-mori.com/researchpublications/researcharchive/ 2215/MFS-Windfall-Survey.aspx

4. S. Agarwal and K. Qian, 'Consumption and Debt Response to Fiscal Stimuli: evidence from a large panel of consumers in Singapore', Institute of Real Estate Studies, National University of Singapore, Working Paper Series (February 2013).

# Verdict: credits and debits

David Ricardo has not left behind an '-ism' as fellow thinkers Keynes and Marx have done, so his importance as an economist rests primarily on his writings about trade. Ricardo was a man of his times and his thinking and writing on issues such as trade restrictions was very much guided by what he saw taking place in post-Napoleonic War Britain. There is no doubt that he was perceptive in seeing that free trade would bring down prices for consumers and would enable societies to get richer as they specialised in what they could do best.

However, the 21st-century global economy is very different from Ricardo's Europe and there is clearly growing resentment at the impacts that Ricardo's free-trade theories have had in practice. Before looking at that it is worth pointing out that his theory has run into criticism by other economists. His critics say that his model only works for two countries trading two goods in a world where there are no disruptions and technological advances. As businesses adapt to either positive or negative shocks they may well stop making and selling the goods they are best at making, either because they no longer have the capacity or because they have decided to focus on something else.

But Ricardian free trade has also been blamed for causing problems that he might not have envisaged. Critics say that specialising in what you do best and leaving everything else to be supplied through imports can lead to unsustainable current account deficits. The massive imbalance between the US and China is a possible example of that. The theory does not take account of different standards that different countries can follow in areas such as pollution and labour standards that will allow one country to secure a trade advantage for all the wrong reasons. Again Chinese industry comes to mind. Critics also say that constantly searching for the right specialisation leads to higher unemployment and greater inequality between and within countries.

# What you should take away

While Ricardo's theories may have dated, he will still hold a place in the economic firmament thanks to some of the ideas that he laid out some 200 years ago:

- Comparative advantage: countries should specialise in what they are most efficient at producing and import goods they are less good at making.

- The Ricardo effect: as wages rise, goods that are produced in a capital-intensive way become cheaper relative to those that were labour intensive, leading to greater demand for the former.

- Ricardian equivalence: governments that borrow to stimulate economic growth will not succeed because people will realise they will have to pay higher taxes in the future to pay back the debt.

# Further reading

Samuel Hollander, *The Economics of David Ricardo* (Heinemann, 1979).

David Ricardo, *The High Price of Bullion, a Proof of the Depreciation of Bank Notes* (1810).

David Ricardo, *Essay on the Influence of a Low Price of Corn on the Profits of Stock* (1815).

David Ricardo, *On the Principles of Political Economy and Taxation* (1817).

# CHAPTER 3

# Karl Marx – the fallen hero?

> 'From each according to his ability, to each according
> to his needs.'
> *Karl Marx*, Critique of the Gotha Programme, *1875*

Karl Marx. Just say his name and almost any listener will immediately conjure up a package of images and thoughts. The famous image of his heavily-bearded face; as the founder of communism; his book *Das Kapital*; the waves of fellow-travellers happy to call themselves Marxists; the Marxist regimes of the 20th century; his tomb in Highgate Cemetery, north London. None of the other nine economists in this book will prompt such a strong and immediate reaction.

One reason is that Marx was not an economist, or at least not just an economist. He was also a philosopher, linguist, revolutionary, and a political campaigner. His fame rests as much on his vision for his political utopia and his writings on sociology as it does on his economic theories. Despite the phenomenal success of his personal brand (albeit after his death), there is a bigger question mark over the long-term impact of his economic theories.

---

*A lot of the nuances of what Marx said and their significance have become lost.*

---

While his thinking may have survived less well than the other economists we have looked at in this book, it is essential to understand what Marx was saying and how his theories were put into practice around the world. The fact that he is such a well-known historical character and the frequency with which his name appears in discussion and debate – often as much as an insult as a cultural reference – means that many people think they know all they need to understand about him. But in fact that ubiquity means that a lot of the nuances of what he said and their significance have become lost.

# Early life and influences

Marx may have devoted his life to understanding the struggle of the working class and plotting its eventual overthrow of its oppressors, but his origins lie firmly in the latter group rather than the former. His life history is as dramatic as that of David Ricardo, but where the British economist enjoyed glamour, his German counterpart mainly saw squalor. He was born in 1818 in Trier, a town in the lower Rhineland in what was then the Kingdom of Prussia. His father Heinrich was a successful middle-class lawyer who ended up owning a number of local vineyards. Heinrich had been born Herschel Mordechai and was the son of the rabbi of Trier but converted from Judaism to the Lutheran faith to avoid the restrictions of anti-Semitic laws.

Thanks to this financial security Karl was privately educated and secured a place at Bonn University to study law, where he lived a life that will be familiar to more modern students. He engaged in duelling fights, picking up a scar in the process, and was joint president of a university drinking club. But as is often the case, his grades suffered as a result and his long-suffering father engineered a move to the more academic and sober University of Berlin.

Marx thrived there academically, passing his law degree. More significantly for his later life he became heavily involved with a school of thought of the German philosopher Georg Hegel. Hegel might well earn a place in a book on great philosophers and his thinking would take up a healthy chapter. But our concern is mainly with a style of analysis that he pioneered, known as the dialectic, through which a thesis is proposed and a counter-thesis put forward, resulting in a new synthesis. While Hegel's followers used this to develop ideas, Marx employed it as a tool to understand the development of the material world and of social revolution.

Marx may have been German but most of his thinking and writing took place in Paris and London. He was accompanied on this itinerant career by his wife Jenny von Westphalen, the daughter of a wealthy Prussian aristocrat who broke off an engagement with a social equal to marry the inferior Marx in 1843. After leaving university he moved to Cologne, where he wrote for, and subsequently edited, the *Rheinische Zeitung*, a liberal newspaper that allowed him to launch attacks on the current governments of Europe.

Under pressure from the authorities, Marx was forced to leave after he wrote an article strongly criticising the Russian monarchy. Tsar Nicholas I successfully pressured the Prussian authorities to ban the publication. In 1843 he went on to Paris, where he contributed to a short-lived liberal paper and met Friedrich Engels, another wealthy middle-class German with whom he would form his main intellectual collaboration. Again his firebrand writing got him into trouble, and the French government expelled him in 1845. Moving to Brussels, Marx and Engels wrote the Communist Manifesto. Marx returned to Cologne to participate in the *Neue Rheinische Zeitung* newspaper, which led to another run-in with the authorities and indeed with his fellow leftists. In 1849 he moved to London, where he embarked on the writing of his three-volume magnum opus *Das Kapital* (*Capital*), only the first volume of which would be published in his lifetime.

Before we leave his turbulent personal life for his writing, it is worth noting the conditions he put himself and his family through in the final three decades of his life (he died in 1883, aged 64). For five years in London, the Marx family lived in a flat at 28 Dean Street in Soho, which is now the kitchen of the high-class London restaurant Quo Vadis (which, as Marx would have known, means in Latin 'Where are you going?'). The coincidence creates two nice ironies for the modern reader.

Marx's life in London, as it had often been on the Continent, can only be described as one of poverty. A Prussian government spy paints a wonderfully yet hideously detailed picture of the Marx household in 1852, describing the main room as full of smoke and tobacco fumes 'that makes your eyes water so much that for a moment you seem to be groping about in a cavern'. He warns that to sit down is a 'dangerous business' as one of the two chairs has three legs while the other (with four) is used as a cooking play table for the children. 'The children's cooking has not been wiped away and if you sit down you risk a pair of trousers.'[1] However, the spy concedes that the friendliness of his hosts makes the 'discomfort tolerable'. Not so for the children. The harsh truth is that three of his children, including his cherished 8-year-old son Edgar, died in that dark abode.

# Economics theories

*Das Kapital*, the book for which Marx will be best known, was the last of the huge volume of writing that he produced and the one that would not be completed until after his

---

1. *Archiv für die Geschichte des Sozialismus*, x (1992), in D. McLellan, *Karl Marx: a biography* (Macmillan Press, 2006).

death. Those who have painfully struggled to read it should remember that the man who wrote it himself suffered almost continuously – although in his case from carbuncles, collections of boils that cause great pain. He was particularly afflicted with carbuncles that grew up on what he calls his 'propagation centre', the agony of which we can only begin to imagine.

The 2,500 pages of *Das Kapital* do merit reading, especially for the sections that are written with a high literary flourish. But to understand Marx's contribution to economics we need to focus on three key ideas: the exploitation of labour that underpins capitalism; that capitalism sows the seeds of its own destruction; and the socialist communist system that will ultimately replace it.

### *Surplus value of labour*

Marx's economic theory is based on the classical economics of Smith and Ricardo. He too looks at commodities and the way that things are produced but comes up with his own theory of value by applying a Hegelian 'materialistic dialectic' to his predecessors' theories. He saw value arising from the effort that the workers put in to produce the goods, as Smith and Ricardo did. But while Ricardo thought that the amount of labour used to make goods determined their prices over the long run, Marx focused on value. In his view the amount of labour determined the value of the good produced. A machine that takes five hours to make something has twice the value as one that takes ten hours. He distinguished between 'use value', which was 'immutable', and the 'exchange value' that the owners of the good could get by selling it.

Marx could see that the workers did not retain all the value of their efforts by a long shot. A machine worker would be paid a wage to produce a box-worth of tools that would sell for a much higher price than his daily wage. Think of a supermarket checkout worker, a solicitor's assistant or a bank teller and you can see that the same dynamic applies now.

Marx saw that there was a difference between what the workers were paid for their efforts and what the factory owners received as a result. Marx called this 'surplus value': the capitalists were able to keep the extra value of profits because they owned the means of production. Capitalists therefore need to pay the workers less than the value at which they planned to sell the goods. This equation also needs to include the costs of the machinery, which Marx explains as being the value of the 'concealed' labour that went in to build the machine. Their profit was the surplus divided by the sum of the labour costs (variable capital) and machines (fixed capital). Marx represented this in Volume III of *Das Kapital* as $p' = s/C = s/(c + v)$ where $p'$ is the profit, $s$ is the surplus value, $C$ is total capital and $v$ is the variable capital.

So how do capitalists know what they can get away with paying their workers? Marx also saw that the factory owners would look to pay the minimum that the workers needed for them and their families to survive – what we would call a subsistence wage. He said that this wage was kept low by the existence of a reservoir of unemployed people ready to take the place of those who could not or would not work. This pool was kept filled by technological advances that reduced the need for labour. Underlying this is the idea that labour is just another commodity that can be bought and sold, with its value being equal to the cost of keeping it for work. It is this difference between labour and what he called labour-value that marks Marx out from the classical economists.

> *It is this difference between labour and what he*
> *called labour-value that marks Marx out from*
> *the classical economists.*

Marx was just as interested as Ricardo was in how economic value was distributed. Ricardo believed the landowners would take the greatest chunk and built his theories on trade reform on those foundations. Marx saw that the capitalists – the owners of capital whether tycoons, financiers or landowners – were the main beneficiaries and believed this system was unsustainable.


## The downfall of capitalism

Since capitalists had a clear incentive to pay workers less, make them work in intolerable conditions and even bring in women and children to do dangerous and dirty jobs, that is what they tended to do. Accounts of industrial life by authors such as Charles Dickens, and Charles Kingsley's *The Water-Babies*, reflect the conditions of the time.

But why would this process simply lead to long-term stable profits for the capitalists? Marx, who was also a historian, saw that social development was in a constant state of flux, with feudalism being overtaken by capitalism that itself would eventually be replaced. Marx said that capitalists would compete, just as Smith said they would, and invest in more machinery to outsmart their rivals.

This is described in one of Marx's more literary passages: 'Accumulate, accumulate! That is Moses and the prophets! Therefore, save, save, *i.e.*, reconvert the greatest possible

portion of surplus value, or surplus-product into capital!
Accumulation for accumulation's sake, production for production's sake: by this formula classical economy expressed the
historical mission of the bourgeoisie.'

The result would be declining profits for capitalists that
would continue to decline as capitalists struggled to stay ahead
of their rivals. Although Marx did not talk in terms of a business
cycle, modern economists would talk about over-investment as
one of the factors that would trigger a bust after a long boom.
For Marx this cycle would continue relentlessly with profits
rising and falling in ever-decreasing circles.

Meanwhile, the growing pool of reserve labour that was
created by this increased mechanisation would both create
unrest and anger against the system and deprive the factories of
potential customers. While the number of tycoons diminished
as they fought for supremacy, so the misery and exploitation of
the working class would increase.

'From time to time the conflict of antagonistic agencies
finds vent in crises. The crises are always but momentary
and forcible solutions of the existing contradictions. They
are violent eruptions which for a time restore the disturbed
equilibrium. With this grows the revolt of the working class,
a class always increasing in numbers, and disciplined, united,
organised by the very mechanism of the process of capitalist
production itself,' Marx wrote.

'The monopoly of capital becomes a fetter upon the mode
of production, which has sprung up and flourished along
with, and under it. Centralisation of the means of production
and socialisation of labour at last reach a point where they
become incompatible with their capitalist integument [skin].

---

*The capitalist system was in Marx's eyes
unsustainable and would end in revolution and
its own overthrow.*

---

This integument is burst asunder. The knell of capitalist private property sounds. The expropriators are expropriated.' Ultimately, therefore, the capitalist system was in his eyes unsustainable and would end in revolution and its own overthrow.

# After the storm: the Communist Manifesto

For the last part in this story we have to go back to Paris in 1848, where Marx and Engels wrote the Communist Manifesto. Unlike today's party manifestos this is a work of literature that takes the reader on a historical tour before embarking on a critique of European industrial capitalism and an explanation of the ideas of labour value and the exploitation of workers by capitalists that are fully fleshed out in *Das Kapital*. It explains that: 'The immediate aim of the Communist is the same as that of all the other proletarian parties: formation of the proletariat into a class, overthrow of the bourgeois supremacy, conquest of political power by the proletariat.' Then, in a manner more familiar to the modern voter, it sets out a ten-point plan:

1. Abolition of property in land and application of all rents of land to public purposes.

2. A heavy progressive or graduated income tax.

**3.** Abolition of all right of inheritance.

**4.** Confiscation of the property of all emigrants and rebels.

**5.** Centralisation of credit in the hands of the State, by means of a national bank with State capital and an exclusive monopoly.

**6.** Centralisation of the means of communication and transport in the hands of the State.

**7.** Extension of factories and instruments of production owned by the State; the bringing into cultivation of waste-lands, and the improvement of the soil generally in accordance with a common plan.

**8.** Equal liability of all to labour. Establishment of industrial armies, especially for agriculture.

**9.** Combination of agriculture with manufacturing industries; gradual abolition of the distinction between town and country, by a more equable distribution of the population over the country.

**10.** Free education for all children in public schools. Abolition of children's factory labour in its present form. Combination of education with industrial production, &c., &c [*sic*].

While the creation of a monopoly state bank and the abolition of private property rights are extreme measures, others would undoubtedly find support among a modern audience, particular free education of all children and the abolition of child labour. But this is a political rather than an economic programme.

So how did Marx envisage the operation of the economy in what the manifesto calls a classless 'association' that has replaced bourgeois society? *Das Kapital* is relatively quiet on that next, vital stage. However, the massive series of notebooks that Marx wrote in 1857 and 1858 in preparation for *Das Kapital*, known as the *Grundrisse*, are more explicit about the socialist communist utopia that would emerge.

According to an analysis of the raw material carried out some 40 years ago,[2] Marx saw six main features of this post-capitalist society.

The most important is the end of the market exchange process as the way to measure values and organise production and, admittedly by implication only, the replacement with some form of socialist central planning.

Second, Marx believed that property ownership would be replaced by ownership by 'associated workers' as the relationship between labour and capital had broken down. Third, a radical reduction of working time and the promotion of disposable social time. Linked to this was the fourth element – the development of the productive capacity of each worker as the measure of their output rather than the value of the immediate work that they do or the amount of hours spent. Science plays a role in the final two elements: a universal development of society's productive forces on the basis of science, technology and automation; and a cultivation of needs on the basis of science and education.

The vision can be summed up as one of communal production where the value of the work is measured by its quality rather than the hours worked, money is a tool for

---

2. J.E. Elliott, 'Marx's Grundrisse: Vision of Capitalism's Creative Destruction', *Journal of Post Keynesian Economics*, Vol. 1(2) (Winter 1978–79), pp. 148–69.

exchange value, and the resulting increase in free time allows each individual to develop in their own way. This is hardly an operational model for running a socialist economy but shows how, in Marx's view, communism would supersede capitalism in a dynamic process similar to the one that saw feudalism give way to capitalism by building on trends established beforehand.

## Karl Marx and the global financial crisis

While Marx might have revelled in the crash of 2008 and mourned the fact that it was the proletariat that bore the brunt of the pain, would his analysis have explained how it came about? The scale of the crash certainly triggered a flow of comments by Marxist economists who also thought the end was nigh for capitalism.

There was a sharp spike in sales of *Das Kapital* in Marx's native Germany, while a manga cartoon version became a best-seller in Japan. Chinese theatregoers flocked to see the most unlikely version of the book – a musical. The show is based around an actor who raises money for a stage play that is then floated on New York's Nasdaq index. The audience members become shareholders and the share price is set by an 'index' of their applause. However, trouble sets in when the 'workers' discover the scale of the surplus value that the play commands over the value of their labour.

One cause of the crash was the boom in complex financial debt products that were based on the growing number of mortgages being given to high-risk poor homebuyers in the United States who were later known as NINJAs – No Income,

No Job, No Assets. Marx would have recognised the desperate search by investors for the high yields that these bonds paid out at a time when interest rates were so low around the world. This idea of the remorseless search for profit at any cost is an integral part of his analysis. He might also see an over-accumulation of surplus capital that would inevitably have led to a bust at some point.

Marx also identified what he called 'fictitious capital', which are paper certificates that guarantee the holder an income stream in the future and can therefore be traded as if they were capital. He said this created an illusion of capital as it was not possible for the capital to exist in the underlying asset. 'Accumulation of money-capital signifies to a large extent nothing else but an accumulation of such claims on production, an accumulation of the market-price, the illusory capital-value, of these claims,' he wrote.

He would have seen that the poor wages of those ill-fated homebuyers were the result of a sustained period of exploitation by the business class. Marx himself saw the potential for financiers – rather than just owners of industrial capital – to extract value from the labouring classes. In the third book of *Das Kapital* he says that the working class is 'swindled ... by the retail dealer who sells them means of existence'. He saw the distinction between selling and loaning as 'quite immaterial'; and that the actions of the lenders were thus a secondary exploitation.

Although governments managed to avert the depression that would have brought about a Marxian end to the last 200 years of industrial capitalism, Marx would have been intrigued by the slow, drawn out nature of the recovery and by the growing anger among populations, especially in Europe. People in countries such as Greece and Spain that suffered from the bust are still suffering. He would see their demands for a new economic system as signs that the battle was not yet over.

# Long-term legacy

The world's economic and political make-up would be very different if Karl Marx had not been born. While many of his ideas were unsuccessful – and sometimes harmful – when put into practice, he has altered the terms of the debate both on a political level and in terms of economic thinking.

## *The big picture*

When it comes to the impact of his economics the influence is less clear. On one level, the end of capitalism that Marx said was inevitable has yet to come to pass. There have, of course, been numerous financial crises as he predicted, including the recent 2007–10 global financial crises. But rather than lead to the decline of capitalism in a spiral of ever weakening growth and wealth, the opposite has been true. Any graph of per capita income in the developed world shows a straight upward line with a few downward blips to mark the Great Depression, World Wars and the recent recession.

As that indicates, workers have become better, rather than worse off, as a result of capitalism. Indeed, it was the stark differences between the wealth enjoyed by people living in capitalist countries and those living under communism that fuelled the overthrow of the latter regime – rather than the other way around.

Working conditions have improved rather than deterio-
rated thanks to innovations such as the minimum wage, which
Marx would have approved of, and trade unionisation, which he
would also have applauded. But what Marx did not predict was
the rise of the middle class, a group of people that did not own
the means of production (unless they bought and held stakes in
Britain's privatised industries) but who could command a high
value for their labour.

Defenders of Marx can point to the fact that governments
of capitalist countries have had to respond to workers' demand
for greater pay and greater rights in order to avert rising anger
and revolution at work as a sign that Marx was on the right lines
in looking at how capitalism would develop as a dynamic model.
The problem is that Marx saw the capitalist system as a fixed
institution that was incapable of change.

---

*Marx saw the capitalist system as a fixed
institution that was incapable of change.*

---

They are on stronger ground when they highlight the way that
rich capitalistic countries have exploited workers overseas, first
via colonisation and more recently through globalisation. While
it is certainly true that inequality has now gone global, this was
not something Marx had in mind when predicting the decline
of the national capitalist systems.

### The smaller picture

But the fact that his predictions were wrong is certainly not the same thing as saying that Marx's thoughts and writings have not contributed to the development of economic theory. There is no doubt that his analysis of the struggle between classes and interest groups within a capitalist system – the Marxist analysis referred to above – is now a mainstream way of looking at social change.

The concept of capital accumulation – the process by which capitalists continued to invest in pursuit of growth to the point at which demand collapses – was a precursor of the idea of the business cycle that moves from boom to bust to recovery to growth and back to boom again.

## *The second coming of Karl Marx*

If Marx could visit 21st-century Britain or America, how would he use his theories to interpret the world as it stands today? His concern that the working class would remain impoverished relative to the capitalist classes does have an echo in the rising inequality in countries such as the UK and the US between those in the top band of society by income and those at the bottom.

While most economists have given up on a labour theory of value, the idea of a surplus value that marks a level of 'exploitation' by business managers of their staff has a very wide currency in today's debates. The idea of measuring the earnings of the top-paid executive in a firm as a multiple of the average level of pay across the company is frequently used to highlight firms with poor pay practices. Companies in all countries still make profits by selling goods and services from more than their input costs, including workers' salaries. As the *Financial Times* reported in June 2013, the pay of the average CEO of a large

US company in 2011 was 508 times larger than that of the average employee.[3]

Marx would undoubtedly get a feeling of schadenfreude from learning about the global financial crisis and the devastating impact it has had on the capitalist economies. Had he arrived at the end of 2008 he might have felt that the final cataclysm was imminent. As time has moved on he would have to accept that capitalism was set for at least another cycle. He would, however, recognise the large pool of reserve labour that had built up in the wake of the crash. According to the International Labour Organisation, a total of 197 million people were without a job in 2012. The existence of the large labour reserve has helped keep wages low: evidence from the UK is that workers have taken the equivalent of a 15 per cent real wage cut between 2007 and 2012.[4]

Had Marx returned four decades earlier, in the 1970s, he would have seen a third of the earth's population run by nominally Marxist governments. It is unlikely he would have been happy. Even in his own lifetime, when confronted by the leaders of a new French Marxist movement he said: 'The one thing I am certain of is that I am no Marxist.'[5] He doubtless would have been appalled that the proletariat in the Soviet Union and countries such as North Korea were dispossessed of both wealth and power.

3. B. Groom, 'ILO reports rebound in CEO pay', *Financial Times*, 3 June 2013. http://www.ft.com/cms/s/0/78568d54-ca19-11e2-af47-00144feab7de.html#axzz2iXfMCG7E

4. R. Blundell et al., 'What can wages and employment tell us about the UK's productivity puzzle?', Institute for Fiscal Studies, June 2013.

5. 'Engels to Bernstein', in F. Engels, *Werke* (Berlin: Dietz, 1956–90), xxxv.388.

# Verdict: credits and debits

There is no getting away from the fact that many of the predictions Marx made about the collapse of capitalism and the rise of the working class have not come to pass. The rise of the middle class across both rich and emerging economies has seen the working class gain a greater share of the means of production without revolution. While Marxism did at one point underpin regimes that ruled a third of the world's population, the collapse of communism in eastern Europe and the Chinese market revolution have left North Korea and Cuba as the sole standard bearers. Ultimately communism could not cope with the underlying human desire for personal and economic freedom.

Nevertheless, the idea that capitalists' relentless search for profit would lead to the collapse of the whole system did appear to have come to pass in September 2008 when Lehman Brothers collapsed. Sales of and interest in *Das Kapital* rose sharply in the wake of the global financial crisis and the failure of mainstream economics to predict or explain the crash. But five years on it seems the world is no nearer a communist revolution than it was in 2007.

---

*Interest in* Das Kapital *has risen sharply in the wake of the global financial crisis.*

---

Marx's last legacy will be as one of the most influential thinkers of the last two centuries. Many historians of modern western thought elevate him as a member of a trinity with Charles Darwin and Sigmund Freud who radically changed how people view the world. To say you are taking a Marxist viewpoint is as effective a piece of shorthand for the speaker as it is to talk about Freudian behaviour or a Darwinian approach.

While much of Marx's writing has not stood the test of time for a majority of economists, *Das Kapital* has moved further up their reading list as the scale of the economic and financial crisis prompted them to go back to Marx's predictions.

# What you should take away

Marx's thinking is still useful as a radically different way of looking at economic relationships. This includes:

- The distinction between a worker's labour and their labour power.

- The idea of the surplus value that accrues to the employer by exploiting the gap between the wages of the labourer and their labour value.

- Capitalists keep wages low to maximise their profit.

- In order to become efficient, capitalists invested an increasing amount of their surplus value in labour-saving machines.

- This leads to the creation of a 'reserve army of unemployed' whose increasing levels of poverty will foment class conflict.

- Ultimately capitalism will sow the seeds of its own destruction.

# Further reading

Karl Marx, *Wage-Labour and Capital* (1847).

Karl Marx, *Manifesto of the Communist Party* (1848).

Karl Marx, *Grundrisse* (1857).

Karl Marx, *Das Kapital* (1867).

David McLellan, *Karl Marx: a biography* (Palgrave, 2006).

Saul K. Padover, *Karl Marx: an intimate biography* (Signet, 1980).

Francis Wheen, *Karl Marx* (Fourth Estate, 1999).

John Cunningham Wood (ed.), *Karl Marx's Economics: critical assessments* (Routledge, 1993).

# CHAPTER 4

# Alfred Marshall – microeconomics arrives

'(1) Use mathematics as shorthand language, rather than as an engine of inquiry. (2) Keep to them till you have done. (3) Translate into English. (4) Then illustrate by examples that are important in real life. (5) Burn the mathematics. (6) If you can't succeed in 4, burn 3. This I do often.'
*Letter from Alfred Marshall to statistician*
*Arthur Bowley, 1906*

Anyone who recoils from economics because of its reputation for complex equations, intricate graphs and unintelligible algebra can probably blame Alfred Marshall. A top-class Cambridge mathematician, Marshall moved over to moral and social sciences early in his career and was determined to apply mathematical rigour to the emerging science of economics.

But he was also adamant that practitioners of economics should explain their thinking and findings in plain English – something some modern-day economists still find challenging. He was determined, too, that economists should strive towards achieving the best outcomes for society, perhaps a reflection of his own humble origins.

But it is for his textbook, *Principles of Economics*, for which Marshall is best known and because of which his place in this book must go unchallenged. He set out core concepts that are essential to the discipline of microeconomics, and therefore to all businesses – supply and demand, marginal utility, elasticity of demand – in such a clear fashion that his book was still the standard textbook for economics students some six decades later.

# Early life and influences

While a modern-day audience relishes a tale of rags to riches, early generations steeped in the Victorian ethos were more likely to paper over any ugly cracks. Thus it is that Alfred Marshall has gone down in the history books as being brought up in a well-to-do middle-class London household. His biography by no less a figure than John Maynard Keynes, an erstwhile student, describes his upbringing in a clerical family from the West Country, in Clapham, a 'leafy London suburb', where his father was a cashier at the Bank of England.

Thanks to the Nobel laureate economist Ronald Coase, we now know that Marshall was a 'master of concealment'.[1] His origins were in the more humble tanneries district of south-east London, Bermondsey, where he was born in 1842 to William, who was a clerk at the Bank of England, and a mother who was a butcher's daughter. His family background was perhaps airbrushed to make it more fitting for the Cambridge don that Marshall would ultimately become.

What is agreed on is that William was a tyrant of a father. Alfred's mother wrote about 'extremely severe discipline' – which for Victorian times must have been something unimaginable to today's children. She recalled how her husband would keep Alfred up until 11 pm to do his schoolwork, with the ironic result that he had to slacken off at school just to keep his wits together.

Although William wanted his son to go to Oxford to pursue a career in the church, Alfred insisted on going to Cambridge to

---

1. R. Coase, 'Alfred Marshall's Mother and Father', *History of Political Economy*, 16(4) (Winter 1984), pp. 519–27.

study maths and was able to do so thanks to a scholarship and, more importantly for our story, through a loan from his uncle, Charles, who had made a fortune in the food and farming business in Australia. The church's loss was economics' gain as Marshall graduated from Cambridge in 1865 with the second highest first-class maths degree – an achievement that earned him the archaic title of 'Second Wrangler'.

But after two years of teaching maths and a quiet drift away from his family's Evangelical Anglicanism towards agnosticism – not fashionable at the time – Marshall became increasingly interested in what was known as moral sciences and rose through the ranks of academia. In 1879 personal life played a role, as his decision to marry Mary Paley, one of his first-class students at Cambridge, meant he had to resign his fellowship at Cambridge. He moved to Bristol, where he became a professor of the nascent subject of political economy at a university that had only opened its door three years earlier. It is significant that Bristol had decided to take in working-class students and to allow men and women to study together.

However, in 1885 Marshall was able to return to Cambridge to take up the chair in Political Economy. The lasting legacy of this personal journey was the separate Economics and Political tripos that he established in 1903. He described this as his most 'cherished ambition'. It led to the creation of the School of Economics at Cambridge that produced some of the dominant thinkers of the 20th century as his book grew in popularity and influence. Perhaps this mix of a Victorian upbringing and signs that he was prepared to challenge the orthodoxy of the time is reflected in the fact that he placed a picture of his 'patron saint', an exhausted, unnamed worker, above his fireplace as a reminder of his vocation to ensure economics improved the lot of everyone.

# Economic theories – supply and demand

We have seen that the debates over a theory of value had dominated early economic thinking from Smith to Marx. Economists had looked at the relationship between the value of commodities and the effort needed to produce them. This is based on the idea that value depended on effort expended in their manufacture or in the labour that went into it. Marshall was among the first to look at how costs and value interacted to determine not only the prevailing market price for a good, but also the amount that would be bought or sold as a result.

> *Marshall was among the first to look at how costs and value interacted.*

Imagine a busy day in a town or city with thousands of people looking to get to work and grab a croissant on their way to the office. If croissants are cheap more people are likely to buy them; if prices are higher – for whatever reason – the number of sales will go down. This will be either because commuters will choose a cheaper alternative or because they want the croissant but cannot afford the higher price (or both). By plotting those changes on the graph at Figure 4.1 with the price on the vertical axis (known as the y-axis) and sales on the horizontal x-axis and joining the dots with a line, it becomes clear that the line slopes down from the top corner (high price, low sales) to the bottom right (low price, high sales).

To understand the impact, it helps to look at this from the bakers' point of view: if prices are too low then they will

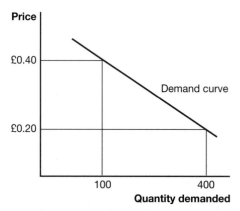

**Figure 4.1   Demand rises as prices fall**

not make many because they will not get back their costs of production. If prices are high they will want to supply as many as they can to boost their revenues. Figure 4.1 shows how the demand side of the equation works. If the shopkeeper cuts her prices (on the vertical axis) more people buy croissants – moving further down the horizontal axis and creating a downward sloping line.

The result is the supply and demand graph wearily familiar to any economics student. Marshall came up with a brilliant metaphor, saying that one might as well argue whether it was the upper or lower blade of a pair of scissors that cut paper as debate whether demand or supply governed value. Figure 4.2 shows the graph from the first edition of Marshall's *Principles of Economics*. This reminds us that it all started there.

The graph, with price on the vertical y-axis and quantity on the horizontal x-axis, shows how the demand line (D) marks the increase in quantity as the price falls while the supply curve (S) shows that the amount supplied rises as the price rises. Where the two meet is the equilibrium. The vertical lines marked R

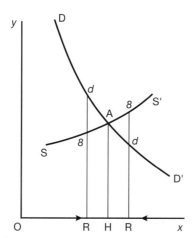

**Figure 4.2   A classic demand/supply graph**
*Source*: Marshall, A., *Principles of Economics*, 8th edn (Palgrave Macmillan, 2013)

show what happens when too little is produced (the price paid [d] exceeds the supply cost [s] so making production profitable and encouraging further production; if too much is produced then the demand price [d] falls below the supply cost [s]).

In a US textbook, by different writers, but also called *Principles of Economics*, one of the co-authors and current President of the Federal Reserve, Ben Bernanke, described Marshall's analysis as 'breathtaking' and said the demand and supply model was 'one of the most useful tools of the economic naturalist'. Marshall has replaced the concept of 'value' with one of 'price'.

# Introducing the concept of time

The clearest indication of Marshall's thinking was the Latin motto that appears at the beginning of *Principles of Economics* – 'natura *non facit saltum*' or 'nature does not move in leaps'. Marshall was interested in biology and often used biological metaphors, partly to win over critics who did not yet see economics as a science. But, more importantly, he saw the important role that time played in this interaction between supply and demand.

If we go back to our busy urban commute, the supply of croissants is effectively fixed by what the shop owners ordered overnight for the morning rush. But if there is a transport disaster on the way into town, many commuters will never make it to work and others will take it as a day working from home. Demand will slump and the town's cafés will either have to dump their stale croissants or discount them. Similarly, if there is a midday power cut across town, workers are likely to stream out of their offices and head for the café. As it is too late to change the supply over this small time horizon – which Marshall called the 'market period' – it is demand that determines the volume of sales and, to an extent, the price. Marshall used the example of fish, which, like croissants, are perishable.

Marshall then looked at what he called the short run (the next week or so, for example). This is long enough for the bakeries to change the amount they supply, either by buying in more dough mixture and hiring more workers, or cutting production by doing the opposite, depending on their evaluation of the market conditions. They can increase supply to meet a short-term spike in demand but only by raising the unit costs of making the croissants (remember Ricardo's diminishing returns from ploughing up new fields). In this case demand and supply interact to set the price.

In the long run the bakeries can invest in more and better ovens and take on more skilled workers, to meet demand fuelled by an advertising campaign or by an increasing reputation of croissants as the 'must-have breakfast'. Seeing a boom other manufacturers will enter the market – perhaps diverting capital towards this more profitable occupation, as Smith foresaw. Both should have the potential to increase supply and reduce unit costs. Here supply affects the price.

# Partial equilibrium – hitting the moving target

Marshall, the amateur biologist, was aware that humans, like animals and plants, adapt their behaviour to changing circumstances. In the case of people there are many factors that might affect their spending and investing decisions. The idea of analysing the stationary state of the economy only makes sense in the 'market period' – the first example of our croissant trade, but before disaster strikes. At that point the market is in equilibrium.

But over the short and long runs, neither buyers nor sellers can be certain about how events will unfold and sooner or later there will be some sort of shock, such as a major drought sending the price of wheat soaring or a terrorist outrage that prompts people not to travel to work or a long-term less dramatic change in costs or demand. At this point all the actors in the economy, realising that things have changed, will change their decisions in a range of ways including buying, producing, investing, hiring and so on. These changes will have knock-on effects across the economy in different ways, and at different speeds and with different intensities.

Marshall realised that this made it pointless to construct a static view of how the economy worked, as all these different factors would impact on each other. The best thing to do, therefore, was to analyse one aspect of this complex relationship to work out what would happen. In order to do this Marshall employs a bit of Latin – *ceteris paribus*, which roughly translates 'as everything else remains the same'.

Using this technique, economists wanting to analyse the impact of a rise in price on demand put all the other factors into what Marshall called 'the pound'. He said this made it easier to analyse the individual reaction, although he admitted it meant the analysis corresponded less to real life. The real advantage was that as the analysis progressed 'more things can be let out of the pound and exact discussions can be made less abstract, realistic discussions can be made less inexact than was possible at an earlier stage'.[2] Other economists had used a *ceteris paribus* idea but it was Marshall who gave it the structure that is still in use today.

## More than just a marginal gain

A vitally important concept that Marshall formalised and which influences microeconomics today is the idea of the marginal change. He did not invent marginal analysis but he applied it in a comprehensive way to analyse how producers and consumers should look at their economic decisions. So what is a margin when it is not the column of white space to the left and right of this paragraph?

In economics the margin is what happens when you take one step further down the road. This may be a decision to

---

2. Alfred Marshall, *Principles of Economics*, 8th edn (1920), Book V, Chapter V.

produce an extra batch of croissants or to raise the price by another 10p or it may be a consumer deciding to have one more croissant even it means busting their diet. In all three cases they can only make a rational decision if they look at the margin cost or benefit that will incur.

The first lesson of marginal analysis, therefore, is that the past is another country. Whatever the supply and demand curves told you about prices and profits up to now will not help in deciding whether to change your strategy. Marginal analysis asks people to think about what they spend their next pound or dollar on, or what they spend their next hour doing. It asks firms to think about whether they want to produce another run of croissants.

> *The first lesson of marginal analysis is that the past is another country.*

A firm should continue making croissants until the revenue that they receive for that final batch equals the cost that has gone into it. At that point the next batch will land them with a loss. Managers therefore have to know what the marginal revenue from that last batch is, and the marginal cost of producing it. The net result is, unsurprisingly, known as the net profit.

A shopper needs to think about how much more enjoyment they will get from buying a bit more. Imagine it is a hot day and you see a bar serving cold drinks. The first drink will be wonderful as it helps quench a thirst and cool you down. If you have a second, that will be nice but not quite as nice as the first. Have a third and you might feel bloated, or if it is alcoholic, a bit worse for wear. While you might have seen the first drink as worth the £2 price the second one might have given you £1.50 of pleasure and so on. You may enjoy each drink but the extra amount of enjoyment you get is slightly less each time. Marshall called this 'diminishing marginal utility'.

As consumers and producers respond to the price signals at the margin, they are likely to change their behaviour. One important way in which they do that is to substitute something that has risen in price – whether a raw material or the final product – with a different, cheaper one. At this point we must put issues like taste and fashion into the *ceteris paribus* pound. This substitution effect, which Marshall was key in developing, is central to understanding how supply and demand change over time. He himself used the examples of coal and charcoal for industry and for domestic heating and barley and sugar for brewing. He also saw that it could be applied to the means of production in cases where the use of machinery would be a better alternative to having large numbers of workers in times of rising wages. As Marshall put it, the principle could be applied to 'almost every field of economic inquiry'.

# Elastic, fantastic: a measure of response

Marshall's understanding of how demand and supply work and how producers and consumers substitute one thing for another, whether coal or charcoal, machines for people, biscuits for croissants or leisure for work, led to the next concept for which he is rightly famous – elasticity. This unusual word is a measure of how responsive people are to changes in prices. If something rises in price will we grit our teeth and buy the same amount or cut our purchases? And if it were to fall suddenly, would we leap in to buy as much as we could?

---

*If something rises in price will we grit our teeth and buy the same amount or cut our purchases?*

---

The answer depends on the nature of the product. Marshall saw there was little elasticity with human necessities. Looking at wheat, the staple food of his time, he realised that a fall in the price would not lead to a sudden rise in demand, as there are not many other uses for wheat than making bread. But people need to eat and so will be prepared to pay more for the amount that they need even if the price rises.

Marshall identified some of the factors that affect the elasticity of demand. One of these is the substitution effect – how easy or difficult it is for us to switch to another good if one rises in price. If croissants spike in price, there are many other delicacies to choose from. If, however, house prices and rents rise, there is no immediate substitute if you wish to stay in the same town. Here again, time comes into the equation as a long-term price rise will encourage people to take more radical substitutes such as living with their parents, cohabiting with fellow workers, moving to a different town if they felt prices were unlikely to fall. Another factor is the buyers' wealth. Marshall saw that rich people could afford to drink wine and would probably continue to do so if prices rose while for poor people it was unaffordable at any price. Finally we add taste into the equation: a 'must-have' piece of technology or fashion accessory.

This allows us to make a small diversion into reverse elasticity. Marshall wrote that his friend Sir Robert Giffen had told him that when the price of bread rose, very poor people in British cities actually bought more rather than less (so that line on our demand graph would slope upwards rather than downwards). As a result, the idea of a good that became more popular when its price rose became known as a Giffen good. Sadly no other observations have been made, other than a complex experiment in China that found that families for whom rice was a staple diet actually bought less when offered coupons allowing them to buy it more cheaply.

# Marshall and the business world

Marshall wrote quite specifically about and for the business audience, which he saw as being the people who would put his ideas into practice and deliver the gains in welfare that he saw as important. In a 1907 essay on 'economic chivalry' he said the resources set free by the 'free enterprise of the strongest businessmen ... would open out to the mass of people new possibilities of a higher life, and of larger and more varied intellectual activities'.

Marshall hoped that businessmen would read his book, but there is little evidence that they did at the time and industrialists were absent among those who praised it. However, his writing sparked a lot of interest in two key aspects of business life: the size of the firm and the idea of industrial districts.

Marshall was way ahead of his time in seeing the importance of geography in economics, a field that has become highly fashionable since. At the heart of his thinking was what he called the 'thickly peopled industrial district' where groups of skilled workers were gathered. These focused on specialised and export-focused activities such as the textiles, iron and steel, and pottery products that he saw emerging in his Victorian Britain. Marshall saw this as a combination of Smith's division of labour, which created internal economies of scale, and the idea of 'integration' or a growth of connections between separate parts of what he called an industrial 'organism' that created external benefits for all those firms involved.

Marshall saw that this organism worked by creating a local market for skilled labour, making it more effective to invest in expensive specialised machinery, as the owners could be confident it would be in constant use to meet the nearby demand. It also created other benefits, which economists would now called externalities. He saw that it would lead to the creation of more ideas and a greater and quicker spread of those innovations. It would also encourage suppliers and other ancillary trades to come to the area.

However, Marshall also saw the vulnerabilities created by the dependency of one area on a single industry because of the dangers of a sudden slump in demand or rise in raw material costs. He was effectively forecasting the impact that the economic turmoil of the 1920s and 1930s would have on industrial areas as the Great Depression sucked demand out of the global economy. It did indeed lead to a flight away from concentrated industrial areas, which were seen as too risky – something that became a 20th-century trend that continued until more modern trends in industrial thinking began in the 1980s.

While Marshall saw the potential strength of industrial districts he also realised that this process of expansion did not – and should not – lead to the emergence of monopolies, although it would lead to the creation of large companies that benefited from economies of scale. He again resorted to a biological analogy, noting how in a forest some trees fail as they are overshadowed by taller neighbours who continue to grow taller until 'age tells on them' and they are overtaken by other new trees. However, he realised that this theory was weakened by the growth of joint-stock companies – what we would now call FTSE-listed plcs – which he acknowledged could secure a 'prominent and permanent place' in the economy.

Marshall saw that these large firms found it easier to maintain their vigour than smaller rivals as they could benefit from both internal economies by exploiting technology and increased specialisation, and external economies thanks to the extra marketing power their size gave them. However, he saw that they would suffer from the problems of being too big, such as expanding into too many areas and adopting overly mechanical systems of administration that suppressed initiative. He did not come up with a full theory for the best size of a firm but he laid the groundwork for subsequent microeconomists to build on.

## Long-term legacy

Marshall developed economics as a science, and his students and later leading thinkers at the School of Economics that he founded, such as John Maynard Keynes, continued that scientific ethos to this day. His concepts of supply and demand as the determinants of price and the graphs that went with them are a lasting legacy of his work. The many business people who have found themselves in front of a PowerPoint presentation over the years can be forgiven for cursing his name!

But his focus on the need for economists to understand how people behave in relation to social life 'as men of flesh and blood … not an abstract or economic man' should not be overlooked. He was ahead of his time in seeing that economic actors should be seen within their social situation. While this perhaps became lost as the concept of rational expectations and 'rational economics man' took over later in that century, in a way it opened the door for behavioural economics.

Marshall's contribution to economic theory is immense. His use of supply and demand as the way to determine prices, and the idea of marginal costs, revenues and utility have now become commonplace tools in economics. While these concepts are normally the domain of economists, all have become part of the language not only of business people and analysts but also, particularly in terms of supply and demand, of the man and woman in the street.

Finally, the whole discipline of industrial economics has its roots in Marshall's thinking on industrial districts, external economies and the firm as an organisation rather than simply an arena for reducing transaction costs. The areas of industrial dynamics, which looks at the growth of capabilities within an industry rather than just a firm, and economic geography, which looks at how economic activity is organised, that feed into today's government business policies, are in part a reflection of the way that Marshall saw the world. The focus on finding a way to mimic the modern high-tech industrial districts of Silicon Glen near Cambridge and the Silicon Roundabout in London's East End reflect his contribution.

Marshall opens *Principles of Economics* with the grand claim that economics is a 'study of men as they live and move and think in the ordinary business of life'. He wanted the book to be read and used by business leaders of his time. There is little evidence that they did, and indeed the only review that historians have unearthed highlighted a minor historical error. However, the influence that his writing has had on later economists, business leaders and policymakers is evidence that he did have the impact he desired, only posthumously.

## Verdict: credits and debits

Although well known in his day, almost a century after his death Alfred Marshall is no longer a household name in the way that Adam Smith and Karl Marx are well established in current popular culture. But his influence continues to resonate through both the academic profession and our daily lives.

Marshall acted as a bridge between the 19th and 20th centuries, in terms of both his lifespan and his development of economic theory. He took the classical doctrine of Smith and others and produced something that is now known as neoclassical economics and set the stage for the battle between Keynes, Hayek and Friedman, whom we shall meet in later chapters. There may not be a doctrine known as Marshallian economics but there would be no economics without Marshall.

## What you should take away

Marshall's influence is clear from the ideas and terminology that he pioneered:

- The use of mathematics in economics and its development as a self-standing science.

- The role of supply and demand as the two scissor blades that determine price.

- The use of graphs as a tool of economic analysis and explanation.

- The partial equilibrium analysis of an economic interaction that parks all other aspects of the economy in the *ceteris paribus* pound.

- The concept of marginalism and the analysis of the impact of the final unit of cost or utility on behaviour.

- The idea of the industrial district and the internal and external economics that drive the development of firms.

# Further reading

Richard Arena and Michel Quéré (eds), *The Economics of Alfred Marshall* (Palgrave Macmillan, 2003).

James Becker, *Alfred Marshall in Retrospect*, New York University, Department of Economics (1991).

Alfred Marshall, *Principles of Economics* (1890).

Alfred Marshall, *The Social Possibilities of Economic Chivalry* (1907).

Alfred Marshall, *Money, Credit, and Commerce* (1923).

# CHAPTER 5

# John Maynard Keynes – the rise, fall, rise … and fall

'This 'long run' is a misleading guide to current affairs.
In the long run we are all dead.'
*John Maynard Keynes,* A Tract on Monetary Reform, *1923*

Of the ten economists in this book, none has enjoyed such
a posthumous revival of interest in their work as Keynes. In
the wake of the global financial crisis which began in 2007–8,
politicians, central bankers, financial analysts and journalists
have all blown the dust off the cover of their copies of his
major work, *The General Theory of Employment, Interest and
Money*, to revisit his lessons from the Great Depression of the
1930s. It was this that provided the furnace in which the British
economist forged his theories.

Keynes's main impact was his theory that justified the
need for state intervention in times of economic depression.
This idea that the government could even out the booms and
busts in the economy was based on a rejection of the core
tenets of the classical and neoclassical economists: that a
free market would always resolve downturns as prices – and
particularly wages – adjusted. It is these two views of the
economic world that take up a large amount of today's public
economic debate.

---

*Keynes's main impact was his theory that
justified the need for state intervention in times
of economic depression.*

---

But it must be remembered that the resurgence in popularity
of Keynes's ideas followed a period when they had fallen out
of favour. This happened after a concerted attack by some of

the monetarists who will appear in the following chapters and an increasing feeling that his theories could not explain the way many economies behaved in the 1960s and 1970s. That argument will doubtless continue over the coming decades, but for now Keynes is at the centre of economic debate.

# Early life and influences

John Maynard Keynes enjoyed a gilded upbringing. He was born in 1883 – just six weeks after Marx was laid to rest. He benefited from a private education that saw him go to Eton College, where he won a handful of prizes, and King's College, Cambridge, where he became president of the Cambridge Union Society. His father was an economist too, but that doesn't tell us the full picture. Had he not been outshone by his son, John Neville Keynes might have been the economist with that surname who would be known to us now. Keynes senior held a lectureship in Moral Science at Cambridge University from 1883 to 1911 and rose to the senior position of university registrar, which he held until his retirement in 1925, aged 73. He wrote a major textbook, *The Scope and Method of Political Economy*, that set out the distinction between positive economics – how the economy does work – and normative economics – how it should work, a key distinction that stands today.

Despite this solid grounding in economics, Keynes junior studied mathematics at Cambridge and was awarded a first-class degree. Ironically it was Alfred Marshall, who had himself won a very highly placed first-class maths degree and who was now a professor at Cambridge, who tried to persuade Keynes to study economics.

Keynes also acquired a great deal of self-confidence from the company he kept. At Cambridge he became a member of the Apostles, a secretive society of the brightest students that discussed intellectual issues of the day. It later hit the headlines in the 1950s when it emerged several people linked to the so-called Cambridge spy ring, including Guy Burgess and Anthony Blunt, had been Apostles. It was there that Keynes met Leonard Woolf and Lytton Strachey, who would go on to become prominent members of the Bloomsbury Group.

Many writers have focused on Keynes's privileged upbringing and concluded that this influenced his optimistic attitude that problems could always be resolved. Harry Johnson, an American academic and chronicler of Keynes's life and writings, has said Keynes believed the government could solve the world's problems – especially if it was staffed with fellow Cambridge graduates! Johnson contrasted Keynes's comfy upbringing with that of Milton Friedman (see Chapter 7), the child of impoverished Jewish emigrants from the Hapsburg Empire, who took an extremely pessimistic view of the role that the state could play in the economy and society, suggesting that it was no coincidence that the two ended up as totems for their respective economic disciples.

# Move into economics: fame and failure

In a move that completed the classic early 20th-century upper-middle-class journey through Eton and Oxbridge, Keynes joined the Civil Service and worked in the India Office (albeit in London) but became bored quickly. He was attracted back to Cambridge by an offer of a lectureship in economics from

Marshall, who had taught him briefly when he was an under-graduate, and took up a lectureship privately funded by A.C. Pigou, Marshall's successor at the university.

However, he had impressed his superiors during his time at the India Office and was appointed as a member of the Royal Commission on Indian Finance and Currency in 1913 at the age of 30 (young for the time). He fought almost a lone battle, even when laid low by diphtheria, to argue against a rigid gold standard for India and for a reserve system that allowed Indian monetary managers to offer a flexible supply of credit. It was clear Keynes saw the role of economics as providing practical solutions to real-life problems even at this early stage in his career.

Keynes returned to Whitehall after the outbreak of the First World War – he was a conscientious objector – and again joined the Treasury, where he was made head of a new section responsible for external finance and in particular for managing the financing of the imports that Britain needed for its war efforts. At one point he managed to corner a supply of Spanish pesetas that were needed to fund imports. While his superiors were delighted, thinking they could now buy the goods they needed, they were shocked to learn that Keynes had sold the money in a successful attempt to trigger a slump in the Spanish currency. This experience of administering external finance would act as a foretaste for his work after the Second World War in establishing the Bretton Woods international monetary system.

After the end of the war, Keynes was appointed the Treasury's official representative at the Paris Peace Conference that was responsible for deciding the level of reparations Germany would pay as part of the Treaty of Versailles. The treaty was signed on 28 June 1919, but three weeks before, on 7 June, Keynes resigned, after it became evident that 'hope could no longer be entertained of substantial modification in the draft Terms of Peace. On Saturday I am slipping away from the scene of nightmare. I can do more good here. The battle is lost.'[1]

Versailles established that Germany had to accept responsibilities for all the loss and damage caused during the war and pay reparations to the Allied Powers that were later put at DM132 billion or $31.4 billion. Later that year Keynes published *The Economic Consequences of the Peace*, a short pamphlet condemning the terms of the treaty in eloquently vitriolic language. It became a best-seller, and largely contributed to the belief that Germany had been harshly treated at Versailles.

Keynes argued Germany should repay $7.5 billion but that the debt should carry no interest and instead be paid in ten annual instalments of $250 million beginning in 1923. In one striking passage he appears to predict the rise of Adolf Hitler and the Second World War. 'If we aim deliberately at the impoverishment of Central Europe, vengeance, I dare predict, will not limp. Nothing can then delay for very long that final civil war between the forces of Reaction and the despairing convulsions of Revolution, before which the horrors of the late German war will fade into nothing, and which will destroy, whoever is victor, the civilisation and the progress of our generation.'

Four years later he again grabbed the public's attention with his book, *A Tract on Monetary Reform*, from which the opening quotation in this chapter was drawn. After savaging the Allies'

---

1. *The Collected Writings of John Maynard Keynes*, Vol. 16, ed. E. Johnson and D. Moggridge (Cambridge University Press, 2012), p. 471.

proposed military solution to the war, he turned his attention to what he saw as the deeply misguided economic policies being pursued by the West's central bankers and finance ministers. One element of this was an adherence to a quantity theory of money – the idea that there is a direct relationship between the quantity of money in an economy and the level of prices of goods and services sold – that first emerged out of the thinking of Adam Smith and David Hume.

By Keynes's time, the theory had developed to state that the quantity of money multiplied by the number of times the money is used must equal the volume of all goods and services sold multiplied by their price. The theory assumes the volume of transactions and the number of times the money is used are not affected by an increase in the money supply. The net result therefore must be an increase in the price level. If the quantity of money in the economy doubles then the price of goods and services will on average double.

Keynes's critique has left us with one of his most famous pieces of writing. He said that while this might be true in the long run it was not necessarily so in the short term. 'In the long run we are all dead. Economists set themselves too easy, too useless a task if in tempestuous seasons they can only tell us that when the storm is long past the ocean is flat again.' He said that 'in actual experience', a change in the money supply was liable to have an impact both on the velocity of any £10 around the economy – and on the real volume of transactions. In his view the quantity of money was not a driving force behind inflation and should be used as a tool to control it.

*Keynes described gold as a 'barbarous relic'.*

This is linked to his second criticism of the decision by western economies to tie their currencies to the price of gold. He believed governments should not engineer deflation in order to bring exchange rates into line with some fixed target. Instead they should devalue their currency, in line with price levels. The nadir of this wrong approach was to tie a currency to the price of gold. It meant a country with a balance of payments deficit would have to send gold to creditor countries. This loss of gold would reduce the money supply and lead to a fall in demand. Keynes described gold as a 'barbarous relic' and urged Britain not to rejoin the gold standard it had abandoned in 1914. When Winston Churchill put the UK back on the gold standard in 1925, Keynes responded with an attack, *The Economic Consequences of Mr. Churchill*, in which he warned that fixing sterling to gold at a rate that was 10 per cent overvalued meant manufacturers would have to cut the costs of production and therefore wages by 10 per cent to compete. The UK left the gold standard in 1931.

While the accuracy of his analysis and predictions brought Keynes fame, his own dealings with money were less of a varnished success. In 1924 Keynes became Bursar of King's College, Cambridge, managing its endowment funds. His performance lagged behind the market in the 1920s, when he used a complicated economic model and a 'top–down' strategy that used monetary and economic indicators to direct his decisions to switch between equities, fixed income and cash. It did not work, and he failed to spot the Great Crash coming and the sharp fall in equities after September 1929. He admitted this approach needed 'phenomenal skill to make much out of it'. However, as we shall see, in this case the long-term was good to Keynes, as was the decision to embrace one of his best-known mantras and to change his mind when the facts changed.

# *The General Theory*: challenging the classical consensus

While the Crash inflicted a brief blow on his reputation as a money manager, the subsequent Great Depression provided the foundry in which Keynes hammered out his masterpiece, *The General Theory of Employment, Interest and Money*. This book pulls together many of the ideas that he set out in his earlier writings – but it goes much further.

The reason for the long-winded title is that Keynes believed he was setting out a whole new theory of economics that would replace the classical and neoclassical versions. It was, in other words, a general theory. To do this Keynes sought to refute two of the key ideas underpinning the classical theory (and perform something of a U-turn from the views he had held in the *Tract on Monetary Reform* that were based on Marshall's thinking and his *Treatise on Money*).

> *The Great Depression showed that, left to their own devices, markets would not self-correct.*

Keynes set out a number of core ideas that drove his understanding about how the economy worked and why classical economics was mistaken. The Great Depression showed that, left to their own devices, markets would not self-correct. Keynes was writing in a period when unemployment in Britain had been stuck above 10 per cent for more than a decade. The idea that all is best in the best of all possible worlds 'provided we let well alone' ignored the impact of a lack of overall demand in the economy. 'There would obviously be a natural tendency towards the optimum employment of resources in a society which was functioning after the manner of the classical postulates,' he wrote with a tone of sarcasm that is heavily embedded in *The General Theory*.

Keynes set out a new way of thinking that introduced new concepts such as the 'propensity to consume', the 'inducement to invest' and the 'marginal efficiency of capital'. Among the many main principles that he sets out in the book, we can focus on four:

- Savings and investment do not always tend to be equal as they are driven by different factors and over different timeframes.

- Output can fall sharply, leaving many people without a job, a situation that cutting wages cannot remedy.

- It is total or 'aggregate' demand in the economy that is key in determining total output, so governments can use tax and spending to boost demand that will boost employment in a depression.

- People's uncertainty and their expectations about the future are key drivers of economic cycles.

### Savings and investment

Classical economics said savings and investment automatically tend to equal each other at every point in time. The key to this equation was the interest rate or the 'price' of money. If consumers saved more, banks would be able to reduce the interest rates they offered, as they would no longer need to use high rates to attract money. Lower interest rates would make it more attractive for businesses to borrow.

Keynes said the decision to invest depended on people's estimate of the difference between the profits they expected to make and the rate of interest they would earn by keeping the money in the bank. Firms' confidence played a key role. They would look to a wide range of factors as well as the interest rate in deciding whether to invest. If they saw households were cutting spending and rebuilding their savings, they would probably not rush out to invest in the face of falling demand. If consumers are cutting spending at the same time as businesses are cutting investment the result is recession.

Keynes pointed out that if everyone took steps to save money this would actually lead to lower aggregate savings in the long run as there would be less economic growth – an idea he called the 'paradox of thrift'. If planned savings exceed planned investments that would lead to a downward pressure on growth, while an excess of investment would stimulate it. It is the instability of investment that is a prime cause of downturns. In its most simplistic form unemployment is caused by a lack of investment.

### Severe falls in output

Keynes says that the impact of a drop in demand will be on the volume of sales rather than on prices (as classical economists thought). If households cut back on spending and businesses reduce investment, there is little that cuts in prices can do to get the economy back to equilibrium. As output falls, this leads to rising unemployment. While classical theory said wages would fall until the economy found a new equilibrium, Keynes said wages would be 'sticky' as workers would not accept real wage cuts, which were not a practical proposition in a world of trade unions, minimum wage laws and jobless benefits.

Besides the practical problems, on a theoretical basis Keynes believed cutting wages would simply exacerbate the downward pressure on output. Since consumers are also workers, if their income falls this means they have less money to spend. As shops and factories see a further drop in demand they will respond, in the classicists' view, by cutting wages further, repeating the process. The solution should be to restore demand. Over the long run the private sector will return but, as Keynes said, in the long run we are all dead. Something a bit more short term and vibrant is needed.

## Aggregate demand and the role of government

That something is the government. Since aggregate growth is made up of consumer spending, business investment and government expenditure – plus the difference between imports and exports – if the first two are declining only the intervention of the third can stop the rot. But Keynes was not an advocate of Marx – he was in fact contemptuous of *Das Kapital*. Instead he believed the state should 'prime the pump', using its economic weight to kick-start a recovery, by encouraging spending and investment that would not otherwise take place. Spending by the state would lead to greater spending by people and thus by businesses, ultimately leading to more people finding a job.

In one of the most-cited passages of *The General Theory*, Keynes says that if the Treasury were to 'fill old bottles with banknotes [and then] bury them at suitable depths in disused coal mines which are then filled up to the surface with town rubbish, and leave it to private enterprise on well-tried principles of laissez-faire to dig the notes up again … there need be no more unemployment and … the real income of the community and its capital wealth also would probably become a good deal greater than it actually is'.

So how does this magic work? At its heart is the idea of the 'multiplier', which Keynes did not invent but can be hailed for making famous. If the government decides to build a power station at a cost of £10 billion, then £10 billion will go into the economy. But what happens to that money? Some of it will go to the workers who are employed as a result. Let's say £5 billion. Keynes said that if people receive some extra money, they spend some of it and save some of it. The amount they spend he called the 'marginal propensity to consume' (MPC) and the amount saved the 'marginal propensity to save' (MPS).

If the workers tend to spend 90p of every £1 they receive then the MPC is 0.9 (or £4.5 billion). Businesses that receive that 90p will spend 90 per cent or 81p (or £4.05 billion). And so on. The mathematical formula for working out the multiplier is to divide one by the MPS, so an MPC of 90 per cent and an MPS of 10 per cent would be a multiplier of $1 \div 0.1 = 10$. A reduction in government spending would have the opposite effect. Tax cuts and increases also have similar, opposite, multiplier effects.

Keynes saw this as a much better way to stimulate growth than cutting interest rates. In a severe depression businesses will not invest however low the rate of borrowing because they are more greatly influenced by other factors such as a pessimistic outlook. In any event governments cannot cut nominal interest rates below zero (otherwise they would have to pay people to borrow from them).

While interest rates may be good at containing an expansion by pulling monetary policy tighter, they are less effective in a downturn – summed up in the phrase attributed to Keynes of 'pushing on a string'. In a depression people will not want to borrow but will hoard money in their banks rather than spend or borrow more. The mere fact that cheap money and cheap labour are available will not be sufficient to make businesses invest and expand if they do not wish to.

### Expectations and uncertainty

If there is one concept at the heart of Keynes's thinking and which marks a break with the classicists it is the role played by people's uncertainty about the future. The belief that markets will return to equilibrium is based on the idea that people will follow their own self-interest and collectively correct any imbalances. This in turn led to the idea that future economic outcomes can be measured, based on a fully informed analysis of past behaviour. Keynes said that uncertainty over the future had a major influence on investment especially where investors were trying to work out what the returns might be over a long time period. 'Our basis of knowledge for estimating the yield 10 years hence of a railway, a copper mine [or] an Atlantic liner amounts to little and sometimes to nothing.'

> *Keynes said that uncertainty over the future had a major influence on investment period.*

Expectations play a large role in Keynes's analysis of investment volatility in stock markets. He says when people allocate some money to savings rather than spending, they then make a second decision. This choice is between cash and other liquid assets such as stocks and shares, bonds and investment funds that allow people to store up money for spending at some future date. He called this the 'liquidity preference theory'.

Keynes said that the 'precarious' nature of stock markets was driven by investors' constantly shifting expectations and valuations, which he said had an 'excessive and even an absurd influence on the market'. He pointed out that investors were not so much interested in what a share might be worth but in how other investors were likely to value it a few months hence. In a famous passage he compared stock-picking with a beauty competition in which the winner is the one whose choice corresponds most closely to the average preferences of all the participants. 'He has to pick not the faces he himself finds prettiest but those which he thinks likeliest to catch the fancy of the other competitors.' Keynes also foresaw what we now call 'herd behaviour' or following the crowds. 'Knowing that our own individual judgement is flawed we fall back on the judgement of the rest of the world.'

To sum up, Keynes was setting out a whole new system for understanding the economic system that broke with the classical school, which he said was a theory that applied only to a 'special case'. He rejected the idea that a laissez-faire economy in which people and firms were left to themselves meant that all that was necessary to restore the economy to full employment was the existence of flexible prices and wages. An economic slump may not be self-correcting as there may be a deficiency in aggregate demand that results in spare capacity or what modern economists call the output gap. There can be limits to the effectiveness of monetary policy in dealing with such a deficiency; and there is an important role to be played by active fiscal policy in stimulating demand.

*The General Theory* was not a best-seller in Keynes's own time, although the author persuaded his publishers to offer the book at the knockdown price of five shillings (25p) to capture what he saw as a popular market. As Professor Paul Samuelson, one of the economists who took on Keynes's thinking, pointed out just after Keynes's death: 'It is a badly written book, poorly organised. Any layman who, beguiled by the author's previous reputation, bought the book was cheated of his five shillings. It is arrogant, bad-tempered, polemical, and not overly generous in its acknowledgments. It abounds in mares' nests or confusions … [but] when finally mastered, its analysis is found to be obvious and at the same time new. In short, it is a work of genius.'[2]

# From national economist to international statesman

The Second World War saw Keynes return to government for his third and most significant session as a public servant. He became adviser to the Chancellor Kingsley Wood, was elected to the Court of the Bank of England and finally elevated to the House of Lords. This gave him unprecedented access to Westminster, Whitehall and the City of London between 1940 and his death in 1946. He was able to apply his thinking to a Keynes plan both for the wartime British economy and for the post-war international system.

---

2. P. Samuelson, 'The Impact of the General Theory', *Econometrica*, July 1946.

Just before he returned to the Treasury he published *How to Pay for the War*, a booklet based on a couple of articles in *The Times* newspaper. From his experiences in the Great War, Keynes saw that rearmament would push the economy past full employment. He advised setting up a compulsory savings plan to take some of the steam out of excess demand in the economy and prevent inflation from attacking the livelihoods of the poorest. The revenue would be used to fund defence spending and be returned in the form of tax credits to people after the war. In other words Keynesian intervention could be used equally to curb a boom as end a depression. The plan was never fully implemented, but Keynes used his role in the Treasury to advocate his policies. This culminated in the 1944 White Paper on Employment Policy that committed the government to 'maintaining a high and stable level of unemployment after the war'.

---

*Keynesian intervention could be used equally to curb a boom as end a depression.*

---

But it was the international economy that was the test bed for the next and final Keynes plan. He saw that out of the ashes of the destruction of the war and the impetus to rebuild there could emerge a new economic order without the deflationary bias inherent in the gold standard that had afflicted the world in the inter-war years. He realised the new order would be led by the United States, as the clearly dominant nation after peace again reigned in Europe and Asia.

Keynes wanted a system that would maintain a balance of payments between countries without the need for nations to endure deflation, high unemployment and indebtedness to achieve that. Ironically the seeds for his vision were sown by the wartime German politician, Walter Funk. What became known as the Funk Plan called for a central European economic block with a clearing union in Berlin that would shield the Continent from the gold standard. While Keynes saw the Nazis would use this to the detriment of their neighbours, he took the idea of using exchange controls rather than currency depreciation.

He devised a system that transferred the burden of adjustment from the debtor nation to the creditor nation (almost certainly the US after the war). His plan envisaged an international currency union that would see transactions that gave rise to surpluses and deficits between countries settled at an International Clearing Bank. It would include an overdraft facility to provide international liquidity to countries that were close to running out of reserves. This would apply the principles of banking – depositors putting spare money into a bank that could be used as loans for borrowers – in an international system. In this the way the creditor would become a part of the solution to debtor countries' problems.

In the context of a post-war era where large areas of the world would require significant imports for rebuilding but would not immediately be able to produce the exports to generate revenues to pay off the debts, it would be the creditor nations that would have to take responsibility for funding the imbalance. Unsurprisingly, given the US was the world's largest creditor, Keynes's American counterpart, Harry Dexter White, proposed a more modest exchange stabilisation fund that could make discretionary loans to troubled countries to prevent them devaluing their currencies and starting an exchange rate war. All members joining this International Monetary Fund would put in an initial subscription (which for the US would be capped at $3 billion).

After two weeks of intense negotiation at the Mount Washington Hotel in July and August 1944 in Bretton Woods, New Hampshire, the US and the UK negotiated a plan that broadly rejected Keynes's clearing union and adopted White's IMF. Keynes did secure the creation of an International Bank of Reconstruction and Development, now part of the World Bank Group, which would focus on economic development, and won some minor concessions. In a touching tribute written a year after Keynes's death, Canadian economist and wartime official William Mackintosh said that Keynes had become 'as he must always have wished, one of the great national forces of England. He had played for England when destiny was at stake.'[3]

# Long-term legacy

As recently as 2007 it could be said that Keynes's 'revolution in theory and policy' was hardly taught in the main university economics schools.[4] Yet just a couple of years later and politicians, economists and the media were queuing up to quote Keynes's writing in support of the stimulus packages being rolled out to prevent the Great Recession of 2008–9 becoming a new Great Depression. And four decades before that President Richard Nixon had declared: 'Now I am a Keynesian.' What caused such a dramatic rollercoaster ride of reputation in the space of some six decades?

In the immediate decades after the war, governments of all political stripes in the market-oriented world tended to

---

3. W.A. Mackintosh, 'Keynes as a Public Servant', *Canadian Journal of Economics*, Vol. 13 (August 1947), pp. 379–83.

4. Paul Davidson, *John Maynard Keynes* (Palgrave Macmillan, 2007).

implement Keynesian policies. Governments played a deliberately active role in economic management. While we cannot prove precise cause and effect – apart from anything else, the world was emerging from a global conflict – the growth rates of the quarter century from 1950 are impressive. Work by American economist Irma Adelman showed that the rich countries enjoyed annual economic growth of 5.9 per cent a year from 1950 to 1973. In terms of GDP per capita – measuring how better off individuals were becoming – the figure was 4.9 per cent for richer countries and 3.3 per cent for developing nations. These were much stronger growth rates than were seen in the Industrial Revolution. Perhaps the high point of Keynesianism was the 1960s when tax cuts proposed by President Kennedy and implemented by President Johnson led to average annual real growth rate of 4.65 per cent from 1963 to 1968 and a drop in unemployment from 6.6 per cent in 1961 to 3.7 per cent in 1968.

## *Keynes falls from favour*

However, economic growth collapsed after 1973 as Keynesian policies failed to provide the remedy to the inflation shocks of the 1970s. These crises gave an opening for the counter-revolution against Keynesianism that came in the form of monetarism. This critique of Keynes's thinking was based on the theories of Friedrich Hayek and Milton Friedman, whom we shall meet in the next few chapters. But, in a sentence, monetarists said that the government was a poor driver of the economy and the focus should go back from worrying about demand to worrying about price – and in particular inflation.

In the subsequent three decades politicians on both sides of the political debate and on both sides of the Atlantic agreed that the government should withdraw from economic management, which should be left to free market forces supported by an interest rate policy aimed at controlling inflation. Markets were again seen to be self-regulating as any shifts away from the equilibrium would be spotted and smoothed out. The apex of this in the world of economists was the Rational Expectations Hypothesis and the Efficient Market Theory.

We will see (in Chapter 7) how Friedman and colleagues at Chicago University and other Midwest institutions led the fight back against Keynesianism with a reversion to the concepts of self-interest and self-regulation that were still dominant in microeconomics. The government, in other words, was part of the problem not the solution. This allowed a wave of policies that pushed back the role of the state, including privatisation, deregulation, tax cuts and weakening of trade union power.

Opponents of Keynes were also able to attack inconsistencies in *The General Theory*. His supporters responded by taking on some the criticisms and updating *The General Theory* to produce what became known as the New Neoclassical Synthesis, which accepted rational expectations but fitted these into the idea of sticky wages. They pointed to imperfect information and advocated limited government intervention to cover the period when markets fail to reduce unemployment.

### *The master returns*

The revival of Keynes can tentatively be dated to 23 October 2008. Giving evidence to the US Congress, the former Federal Reserve chairman Alan Greenspan said he had 'found a flaw' in free-market economic theory. He said: 'I made a mistake in presuming that the self interests of organisations, specifically banks and others, were such that they were best capable of protecting their own shareholders and their equity in the firms when a massive earthquake reduced the financial world to rubble.'

The Efficient Market Hypothesis (EMH) could not explain how financial markets had moved so far out of line and had perhaps lulled investors into a false sense of security. Instead economists looked at the role uncertainty played in encouraging investors to engage in financial speculation that eventually led to instability, as Keynes had said it would. The decision by the American, British and German governments to use public money to shore up failing banks offset the private sector's desire to hoard cash and liquid assets.

Economists at the time said that the crash could both be explained and resolved by following *The General Theory.* Politicians meeting in London a year later for the G20 cited Keynes specifically – the then Chancellor, Alistair Darling, said that 'much of what Keynes wrote still makes sense'[5] – while the G20 unveiled plans to inject billions of dollars of public money into the economy to offset the slump in consumer spending and business investment that was sending unemployment soaring.

While the precise causes of the global financial crisis that began in the sub-prime US housing sector and spread across the western financial system are still debated, modern Keynesians pointed to a mispricing of risk that the EMH had not corrected. Rather financial markets had been caught up in a crowd mentality. Meanwhile three decades of financial deregulation had increased the risk of instability to the real economy. As Keynes said: 'The practice of calmness and immobility, of

---

5. http://www.guardian.co.uk/politics/2008/oct/20/economy-recession-treasury-energy-housing

certainty and security suddenly breaks down. New fears and hopes will, without warning, take charge of human conduct.' His liquidity preference theory also seemed to explain the flight by investors into cash as they lost confidence in the ability of their investments to make a profit.

Another cause of the crisis is likely to be the huge imbalance between savings and investment due to the amassing of reserves by China and other Asian nations, particularly of US dollars. In the run-up to the crisis concern over the deficits in the US and Europe and the surpluses in China were downplayed. In the wake of the crisis attention focused on the use of capital controls, something Keynes advocated, to curb potentially destabilising investment flows.

However, it was in the response to the crisis that Keynes was most visible. Political leaders and the head of the IMF started calling for a coordinated global stimulus package to prevent a further deterioration in the world economy. The leaders of the G20 countries participated in stimulus measures that were worth about 2 per cent of global GDP and a major easing of monetary policy. The moves were widely credited with averting a depression and for putting the foundations in place for an economic recovery that began to emerge in 2010.

### The revival fades

However, as the economies of the world began to recover, enthusiasm for following Keynesian policies faded. Many governments had already started to withdraw fiscal stimulus measures in 2010 when the sovereign debt crisis in Greece in October of that year put the focus on the perceived need to cut public spending and raise taxes to bring national deficits across Europe under control. The scale of the fiscal stimulus left countries with large debts that they are rushing to pay down. As Keynes's chief biographer, Lord (Robert) Skidelsky, has said, the 'stampede to austerity, before recovery is secure, is depressing testimony to how skin-deep the revival of Keynes has been'.

---

*As the economies of the world began to recover, enthusiasm for following Keynesian policies faded.*

---

There has also been a growing hostility to greater government influence both in the economy and in financial regulation. Within academia there has been a vigorous argument between Keynesians who say that adherence to his policies helped save the economy and will help deliver sustainable growth, and monetarists who say that billions of pounds and dollars of wasteful government spending has held back the private sector recovery and left taxpayers nursing heavy debts.

On a final note it is worth recording that Keynes success-fully put his money where his mouth is. Despite the setback to his investments during the Great Crash, his 22-year tenure as Bursar of King's College, Cambridge was successful and saw him deliver an extremely strong return. According to two academics at Cambridge's Judge Business School, every £100 Keynes invested at the outset would have been worth £1,675 by his death in 1946.[6]

---

6. James Chambers, Elroy Dimson and Justin Foo, 'Keynes the Stock Market Investor: the inception of institutional equity investing' http://ssrn.com/abstract=2023011

# Verdict: credits and debits

Keynes is clearly one of the two most important economists of the 21st century. However, his ferocious battle with monetarists such as Friedrich Hayek (see Chapter 6) and Milton Friedman (see Chapter 7) means that any judgement either positive or negative will not go unchallenged. Nevertheless we can set out some claims.

The first is that he helped defend and save capitalism at a time when it was under threat from both fascism and communism by showing how the state could play a benign and positive role in economic management. Secondly, he established the concept of macroeconomics as the study of how the economy as a whole operated, rather than of the individual firms, consumers and workers within it, and therefore the design of models for solving macroeconomic problems. The third, which flows from this, was the idea of constructing national accounts, which has enabled economists since to build economic forecasts thanks to the fast-growing array of statistics now available. Fourth is the growth of development economics and the focus on policies that can help poor countries achieve higher levels of per capita growth thanks to well-targeted government interventions. Finally his thinking on how to manage international capital flows and debts is likely to continue to inform the debate as policy-makers struggle to agree on a new framework in the wake of the financial crisis.

# What you should take away

John Maynard Keynes has had a lasting impact both on theoretical economics and on the tools that policymakers can use to run their economies in good times and bad. Some of his important ideas include:

- His prediction that the reparations demanded by the Allies after the First World War were so large they would leave Germany perpetually poor and, therefore, politically unstable.

- His introduction of the concept of aggregate demand as the sum of consumption, investment and government spending.

- The idea that full employment could be maintained only with the help of government spending.

- The paradox of thrift that if everyone tries to save during a recession the effect will be to cut consumer spending, leading to job losses and business failures and a worse recession.

- The multiplier effect that says government spending of £100 that boosts people's incomes will have a greater economic impact as those people will spend more money, so creating more jobs.

- Wage stickiness – the idea that workers will refuse to accept cuts in their wages.

- His work, *The General Theory*, is considered the foundation of modern macroeconomics.

- The Keynesian school of economic thought, which takes his name, is one of the principal doctrines taught at colleges and universities.

# Further reading

Paul Davidson, *John Maynard Keynes* (Palgrave Macmillan, 2009).

Dudley Dillard, *The Economics of John Maynard Keynes* (Prentice-Hall, 1948).

J.M. Keynes, *The Economic Consequences of the Peace* (1919).

J.M. Keynes, *A Treatise on Money* (1930).

J.M. Keynes, *The General Theory of Employment, Interest, and Money* (1936).

J.M. Keynes, *How to Pay for the War* (1940).

J.M. Keynes, *Economic Possibilities for our Grandchildren* (1980).

Lorenzo Pecchi and Gustavo Piga (eds), *Revisiting Keynes* (MIT Press, 2008).

Robert Skidelsky, *John Maynard Keynes*, 3 vols (Macmillan, 1992–2000).

Robert Skidelsky, *Keynes: the return of the master* (Penguin, 2009).

CHAPTER 6

# Friedrich Hayek – the archetypal libertarian

'The curious task of economics is to demonstrate
to men how little they really know about what they imagine
they can design.'
*F.A. Hayek,* The Fatal Conceit, *1988*

It was an intellectual battle that has reverberated through economics, politics and philosophy – and even rap music – right through to the present day. Even as Keynes was busy in Cambridge formulating his General Theory, his ideas were being challenged by an Austrian economist who had moved to London, would later take British citizenship and ultimately earn the Nobel Prize for his thinking that ran wholly contrary to that of his adversary.

The philosophy Hayek set out sought to repudiate the principles not just of Keynesianism but also of socialism and any other -isms that looked to government to play a major role in the running of the economy or of society. He saw open and free markets as not just the most efficient way of organising economic activity but as a guarantor of personal liberty. While Keynes is certainly the best economist of the first half of the 20th century, many would hand that title to Hayek for the second half.

# Early life and influences

The early personal life of Friedrich August von Hayek, or F.A. Hayek as he was better known, is uncannily similar to that of Karl Marx. Both were born in that vast swathe of middle Europe around modern-day Germany, Hungary, Austria and Yugoslavia that had been – and would continue to be – heavily fought over. They both had connections with nobility and both made their names in London. But there the similarity ends. While Marx is seen as the father of communism, Hayek was one of the great defenders of personal liberty of the last century.

Hayek was born in 1899 in Vienna in what was then the Austro-Hungarian Empire into a family that had risen up the class system to have reached the lowest level of nobility – thus the 'von' (equivalent to 'sir' in modern-day Britain) that would have appeared in his name until titles of nobility were banned in 1919. He moved in auspicious circles: the Wittgensteins were distant cousins and family acquaintances and Hayek became friends with the philosopher Ludwig Wittgenstein. Hayek later said that his fellow Austrian's philosophy and methods of analysis had had a significant influence on his own life and thought.

The young Hayek served in the First World War, joining an artillery tank regiment in 1917 that fought in Italy. Hayek said his war experience was a 'decisive influence'. Serving as an Austrian officer in Italy, he recalled that he fought in a battle in which 11 different languages were spoken. 'It's bound to draw your attention to the problems of political organisation.' Hayek then decided to pursue an academic career, determined to help avoid the mistakes that had led to the war. He pledged to work for a better world and continued to do so into his nineties. It was also during the war that Hayek was introduced to books on economics, given to him by a fellow officer, and came across both socialist and anti-socialist propaganda.

After the First World War, Hayek earned doctorates in law and political science at the University of Vienna where he also studied philosophy and economics and was immersed in a liberal stream of teaching. While he was there he took part in the private seminars organised by Ludwig von Mises, the last member of the Austrian School of Economics. It was this school which pioneered thinking on the dominant role that individual choices play in the economy and in explaining business cycles – two concepts that Hayek would take on and develop in great detail. These seminars, which also included a number of bright young economists of the time who would go on to make their names in their own ways, in a way matched Keynes's Cambridge 'Circus'.

Aged 28, Hayek was appointed director of the Austrian Institute for Economics Research, where he stayed for four years, lecturing at Vienna University, until in 1931 he was lured by Lionel Robbins, an opponent of Keynes, to join the London School of Economics as professor of economic science and statistics, a post he held for almost 20 years. Unable to return to Austria after the Nazi invasion, Hayek took British citizenship in 1938 but after 1950 lived in the United States and then Germany, where he died in 1992.

# Key economic theories

Hayek was an active thinker and writer and he published books and articles for almost 60 years between 1929 and 1988. Over that period he developed ideas on a range of subjects. But four areas stand out as having an importance and influence that have continued beyond his lifetime. These are:

- an explanation of the business cycle;

- the subsequent battle royal with Keynes;

- the role of prices in communicating knowledge;

- his opposition to central state planning on both a philo-sophical and economic basis.

## Boom and bust/Squaring the business cycle

As a free-market economist Hayek subscribed to the view set out by Adam Smith that the economy was driven by the collective power of thousands or millions of decisions by individual consumers, shopkeepers and factory owners. But if that were always the case at every moment in time there would never be a hiccough in growth. So how can we explain that?

Hayek could see that economies did not follow a straight line but moved around in swings of boom and bust. His business cycle theory was based on the idea of a 'natural rate of interest' – the rate at which savings should equal investment. At this point the economy would be in equilibrium. At different times in the business cycle the market rate of interest – the cost of borrowing that people use – either rises above or falls below the natural rate and the economy moves out of equilibrium.

> *Hayek could see that economies did not follow a straight line but moved around in swings of boom and bust.*

Periods of excessive credit and over-investment meant that monetary policy was too loose and investment would continue to rise as businesses sought to take advantage of future profits. Hayek saw two factors that would trigger an acceleration in economic growth above that flat steady path, and which ultimately would end in a bust that would be followed by a recovery leading to a new cycle. Unsurprisingly, the blame for both ultimately falls on the central authorities.

In his first explanation, central banks at times expand the money supply too quickly, bringing down the cost of borrowing and so igniting an investment boom as people and firms take advantage of cheaper money. The second explanation is a little more complex. Hayek saw that at times businesses would become more optimistic about the economic outlook, perhaps due to a technological innovation, and so would want to borrow more money to invest in their firm to take advantage of this perceived boost in future spending. In order to prevent this demand for credit driving up interest rates the central bank now creates more credit to keep a lid on borrowing costs.

In both cases Hayek said that this credit expansion by the banks generated excessive investment that was directed towards inefficient uses and which would have to be corrected in the bust phase. The decision by the central bank to expand credit – perhaps as a result of political interference or miscalculation by the bank itself – encouraged investment by bringing down the interest rate, which would normally rise to act as a check on borrowing.

### *Time is money*

In order to see how the move away from the natural state would affect the economy, Hayek developed a theory of how the production process worked. Time is an important element in Hayek's thinking about the role that capital – the stock of machinery, buildings, vehicles and other assets used in the business process – plays in the economic cycle. He saw that capital had a different value to businesses in different parts of the economic cycle and that it was the constant attempt to find an equilibrium that caused business cycles and unemployment.

In the scenario where there is an increasing supply of credit and a fall in the market interest rate below the natural rate, investment plans that were not affordable suddenly look profitable with lower interest rates. Long-term capital-intensive projects look more attractive than short-term labour-intensive investments because a lower interest rate is a much more important factor for investments that require borrowing over many years (this is well known to professionals as the discount rate used to calculate future projects in today's money). Hayek was worried this would draw money and other resources such as labour away from more traditionally priced sustainable projects towards these long-term investments. Because long-term projects require continued investment over time they push up the prices of raw materials, equipment and labour. Economists call this 'crowding out' and a good example from modern times is the proposed High Speed 2 fast train line from London to the North, which critics say would both pull resources away from better, smaller projects and lead to a spike in salaries for engineers and other skilled staff.

This leads to interest rates rising to match the surge in demand for credit.

Eventually the demand for credit would push up interest rates to a level where they are unaffordable or central banks would finally act to tighten monetary policy, bringing the expansion phase to an end. Those long-term capital projects (such as the railways in the 19th century, cars in the 20th and the internet-based innovation investment at the turn of the millennium) would become unprofitable and would suddenly become uneconomic. This would mean that the large volumes of intermediate goods that had been ordered and produced to meet the expected long-term demand, such as parts for cars and trains, rail tracks and sleepers, would no longer be needed and the costs would have to be written off. Money then moves into production processes that can be carried out more quickly with a lower debt burden. Workers would lose their jobs as businesses struggled to adapt to the new production processes.

Given that Hayek was setting out his theories in lectures and writing in the early 1930s when the world was heading into depression, it is interesting to see how his theory can explain what remains the biggest business cycle in economic history. Hayek observed that the 1920s boom that led up to the bust was a period of innovation, investment and rising prosperity. The boom led to a surge in investment in long-term, more specu-lative activities all financed by credit-creation by the banking system, until a rise in borrowing costs brought the boom to a shuddering halt. He blamed policymakers for not shutting off the credit tap earlier. But once the crash had become the inevi-table consequence Hayek believed that it needed to be allowed to self correct rather than the government stepping in, which he argued would only prolong the agony.

Hayek set out his thinking on the business cycle, the role of money and his theory of capital in *Prices and Production*, a book published in 1931 and based on his series of lectures at the London School of Economics. It was as a result of that he was offered the Tooke chair in economic science and statistics and turned the LSE into a centre of free-market thinking.

## Hayek vs Keynes

Since Hayek saw that adjustment process as both inevitable and necessary to bring the economy back into equilibrium, he believed that any attempt to intervene would simply push the economy further out of equilibrium and add fuel to a boom that would ultimately lead to an even more devastating crash than before. Instead the right response is to allow the production side of the economy to adjust. In modern language, Hayek was looking to the supply side of the economy.

Given that he was writing at the time that the economy was sliding into a depression, this ran counter to a growing public demand for action to revive the economy and stem the rising jobless total. As we saw earlier (in Chapter 5), Keynes and his Cambridge Circus were in the vanguard of the academic argument for focusing on what we now call the demand side of the economy.

Keynes believed that the problem at the heart of a recession was that resources were not fully used as there was not enough demand in the economy. The solution therefore was to intervene to stimulate demand. He said that cutting interest rates and boosting government spending would alleviate the recession and trigger recovery. Hayek on the other hand believed the economy tended towards full employment but the problem was misallocation of those resources. Hayek believed Keynesian policies to support employment would lead to higher and higher inflation.

*Hayek believed Keynesian policies to support employment would lead to higher and higher inflation.*

This disagreement has become known as the clash that defined modern economics. Keynes won the battle thanks to his greater ability to convey his message to the public and politicians and to the fact that his theory aimed both to explain the mass unemployment sweeping the world *and* to offer a solution. Hayek failed to challenge Keynes's overall vision but instead concentrated his attacks on perceived failures in Keynes's academic thinking.

In 1931, Hayek delivered a lecture in Cambridge at the invitation of his Keynesian critics that was received in stony silence. One of them asked why if in the middle of a slump he went out and bought a coat he would not help to increase output and employment. Hayek replied that it would take a long mathematical demonstration to explain why not. As Keynes's biographer Robert Skidelsky has put it, his hero won because 'he had put forward arguments that seemed more relevant for dealing with a depression that was in full swing'. By the end of the 1930s even the LSE was Keynesian. 'As Nature's cure failed to produce recovery, Hayekians deserted to the Keynesian camp,' Skidelsky said in 2010 in a lecture at the nadir of the European crisis.[1]

While Hayek's hostility towards any form of central planning was the logical deduction from his theories about the way that markets operated, this thinking was developed later in his life after he had moved away from pure economics in favour of political philosophy. The reason for this change of emphasis relates to an intellectual battle fought between Hayek and Keynes and by their supporters in the decade leading up to the Second World War. At the start of the 1930s the two men were developing very different theories about how the economy worked. Yet by the end of the decade Hayek was no longer seen

---

1. Robert Skidelsky, 'Interpreting the Great Depression: Hayek versus Keynes', prepared for the INET Conference, Cambridge University, 8–11 April 2010.

as being at the vanguard of economic thought and would fall out of favour for the next few decades.

## Out of fashion

In 1937 Hayek published an article on the free market and knowledge, *Economics and Knowledge*. It set out his thinking on the important but more abstruse subject of how individuals use knowledge, but by the time it appeared Keynes and his *General Theory* were the talk of the town and his call for the state to intervene in times of recession was on everyone's lips. Hayek's article, which was based on his presidential address to the London Political Economy Club the previous year, refers only to the Great Depression as 'those intertemporal price relationships which have given us so much trouble in recent times'. Hayek believed the priority for economists was to understand how the economy achieved equilibrium as a result of millions of decisions taken by people, many of whom were acting on the basis of little information. Economists should therefore intentionally blind themselves to concerns over how to deal with what was going on in the economy right now and certainly not try to intervene.

Despite this image of a public clash, Hayek and Keynes never debated the issue head-on but instead locked horns in a series of letters and reviews of each other's works. The argument kicked off in 1931 when Hayek was urged by Lionel Robbins to review Keynes's *Treatise on Money* in the journal *Economica*, which Robbins edited. It is hard to overstate the degree of contempt that the 32-year-old Hayek shows for his senior rival in the review. Choice phrases include claims that the work is 'avowedly in an unfinished state', 'unintelligible to those who are not experts' and contains a 'degree of obscurity which is almost unbelievable'.

Keynes could not let the matter rest but instead decided to attack the 26-page review head-on, perhaps because, as he admitted in his response, Hayek had sparked his curiosity. In response he gave as good as he got, describing Hayek's *Prices and Production* as a 'frightful muddle' and as an argument that ended 'in Bedlam'. The two chose arguments over technical definitions as their theatre of war, and both seemed annoyed that the other had failed to see the broader picture they were setting out. Keynes believed the reason Hayek seemed to misunderstand his ideas was that his rival was too locked into the Austrian School theories of the previous century.

Hayek wrote a riposte to Keynes's critique that maintained the high-octane temperature of the debate, prompting Keynes to respond with a short personal note seeking clarification. This led to a hectic flurry of letters often by return of post with each seeking and responding to queries over the definitions they used.

Hayek then published a second long attack on Keynes in 1932, this time focusing on Keynes's public appeals to intervene in the economy to tackle high unemployment. Keynes had used a 1931 BBC broadcast to urge 'patriotic housewives … to sally out tomorrow early into the streets and go to the wonderful sales'. Finally Hayek attacked Keynes's argument directly, saying any attempt to increase investment to match savings that households were making during the downturn would simply lead to inflation, misdirection of production and ultimately another crisis.

Keynes did not respond. He had moved on and was focused on writing the *General Theory*. Instead he persuaded his Cambridge disciple Piero Sraffa, an Italian economist, to review *Prices and Production* in the *Economic Journal* of March 1932. The review angered Hayek enough for him to write a strongly worded rejoinder and soon the Italian and Austrian were joined in battle. As governments followed Keynes's advice during the war and, after his death in 1946, Keynesian economics became the dominant theory over the following decades, both Hayek and his battle with Keynes faded from memory.

## Prices and knowledge

Away from this hurly-burly, Hayek was fascinated by the role that free markets played in distributing knowledge to those whose decisions would be based on their use of that knowledge. He set out to explain how a combination of 'fragments of knowledge existing in different minds' brings about results which, if they were to be brought about deliberately, would require a knowledge on the part of the directing mind which no single person can possess.

---

*Hayek believed that there was no such thing as objective 'data'.*

---

Hayek believed that there was no such thing as objective 'data'. Instead these facts on which people made their decisions were the ones present in their mind at that time. The free market is not a fixed idea or institutions but something that developed spontaneously. The way that the economy developed was therefore as dependent on a division of knowledge as on the division of labour that Adam Smith set out.

It is a complex system in which millions of consumers and producers armed with types and quality of information carry out transactions with others that in turn send new signals and add to people's knowledge. In Hayek's view, the price mechanism of the free market is a powerful tool to enable people to overcome the fact that they do not have perfect knowledge. Each change in price gives people new information to incorporate as they seek to make the optimal decision for themselves. The key dictation is that the market equilibrium is a *process* not a *state*.

The end result is not the perfect free-market solution which assumes that every price set by consumers and firms is correct and that the economy will move towards some perfect equilibrium. Hayek believed that the price reached through competition was determined by the interaction between supply and demand at that point and was not a given fact. Each price that is set is the result of imperfect knowledge and can be overtaken as new information emerges.

The important distinction between Hayek's view and either perfectly rational or planned alternatives is that the free market is 'the result of human action but not of human design'. He believed it was a mistake to think that economists could understand economies in the same way that scientists can explain the physical world. According to Hayek, a market system is a discovery technique. No computer can predict the emergence of new knowledge, original ideas or innovations – and people's reactions to them.

Individual participants do not need to have all the available knowledge to take the right action for them. This means people will act in different ways according to the knowledge they have. While this might seem chaotic and uncoordinated, the net result was the most efficient allocation of resources given the available knowledge at that precise moment. Order would emerge spontaneously from chaos. Hayek said the price system was 'a kind of machinery for registering change, or a system of telecommunications which enables individual producers to watch merely the movement of a few pointers, as an engineer might watch the hands of a few dials'.

Hayek used the example of a sudden shortage of tin. This could happen because of a surge in demand due to a new use for the metal, or because of a major supply problem. He said that people who needed tin did not need to know which reason was right. The rise in the tin price alone told them that they only needed to know they had to cut down on their use of tin and find substitutes. Those businesses that saw that they could make money by offering substitutes for tin would fill the gap without needing to know why it had occurred.

The effect will rapidly spread throughout the whole economic system and influence not only all the uses of tin but also those of its substitutes and the substitutes of these substitutes, the supply of all the things made of tin, and their substitutes, and so on, Hayek wrote.[2] 'The whole acts as one market, not because any of its members survey the whole field, but because their limited individual fields of vision sufficiently overlap so that through many intermediaries the relevant information is communicated to all.' Hayek believed that prices sent signals to decision-makers that could not otherwise be delivered and that open competition was both the best way to ensure the economy moved towards equilibrium and the best incentive for innovation.

---

2. F.A. Hayek, 'The Use of Knowledge in Society', *The American Economic Review*, Vol. XXXV(4) (September 1945), pp. 519–30.

### Anti-central planning

The culmination of his examination into how an economy worked, his faith in a self-correcting mechanism and the idea of the free market as the most efficient way to allocate resources were brought together in what is undoubtedly Hayek's most enduring contribution to economics and political philosophy. This thinking provides the underpinning to an assertion that rests at the core of Hayek's philosophy: that it is the free decisions of individuals that leads to the best allocation of resources and that intervention by governments only distorts the economy, at best, and leads to dictatorship, at its very worst.

---

*It is the free decisions of individuals that leads to the best allocation of resources.*

---

The initial step in this intellectual process was to challenge the idea that central planning could deliver a better outcome than the collective weight of decisions taken in a free market. In particular Hayek wanted to counter the then popular idea that socialism could use the market mechanism to achieve those results – known as socialist calculation. He said the knowledge planners needed to make their decisions did not exist in a vacuum but was the result of the market interactions. Planners who based their decision on a snapshot of information would find their decisions quickly obsolete. How, in Hayek's view, could one person's knowledge ever surpass the total weight of the million different pieces of knowledge held by various people in the economy?

But it was his application of this thinking to the broader political arena that brought him wider fame and is the reason why his name will be remembered in years to come. The enthusiasm for central planning in Britain as a way to restore economic growth after the end of the war horrified Hayek, who saw it simply as a precursor to the totalitarian systems that he witnessed in Nazi-occupied Austria and which were now dominant in the Soviet Union. He set out his thoughts in the book, *The Road to Serfdom.*

While his previous writings had argued that free markets lead to increased economic efficiency and so greater prosperity, Hayek now extended this argument to say that they helped safeguard liberty. The book was published in the UK and the US in the final years of the Second World War and, despite paper rationing in Britain, became a best-seller. Hayek was clearly aware it would become a significant document. He says in the introduction that writing the book was 'a duty which I must not evade' but which would 'offend many people with whom I would wish to remain on friendly terms'.

The book is a political work, arguing for a lesser role for government in society and the economy. Hayek says that when the state undertakes direct control in fields where there is no voluntary agreement by everyone in society, it is bound to suppress individual freedom. 'Once the communal sector, in which the state controls all the means, exceeds a certain proportion of the whole, the effects of its actions dominate the whole,' he says. He was worried that even in democracies there was a growing tendency to hand over decision making to 'experts, permanent officials or independent autonomous bodies'. 'In these instances delegation means that some authority is given power to make with the force of law what to all intents and purposes are arbitrary decisions.'

State planning, he said, necessarily involves deliberate discrimination between particular needs of different people, and 'allowing one man to do what another must be prevented from doing'. Ultimately, allowing the state to take more decisions over our lives, such as what job we do and how much we are paid, would give it complete power to decide what we are to be given and on what terms. 'What matters is that we have some choice, that we are not absolutely tied to a job which has been chosen for us, and that if one position becomes intolerable, or if we set our heart on another, there is always a way for the able, at some sacrifice, to achieve his goal. Nothing makes conditions more unbearable than the knowledge that no effort of ours can change them.'

Hayek did see a role for the state but one that was confined to establishing rules applying to general types of situations and left everything else to individuals' freedom. He took a similar view of the state as Adam Smith, saying its institutions should support aspects such as the role of law that would underpin free and fair trade, and public services such as roads that could not be funded by individuals. Hayek was, however, in favour of governments providing a generous safety net for the less advantaged, including a home for every citizen and universal health care. But his message was clear: 'Individual freedom cannot be reconciled with the supremacy of one single purpose to which the whole society must be entirely and permanently subordinated.' In his final work, *The Fatal Conceit: the errors of socialism*, published in 1988 when he was 87, he laid out how he believed that western civilisation had erred in embracing central planning and forsaking respect for the individual and their decisions as the foundation of freedom. 'The dispute between the market order and socialism is no less than a matter of survival.'

# Long-term legacy

Four decades ago few people outside the academic community would have recognised Hayek's name. Indeed, when Hayek was awarded the Nobel Prize in 1974, Paul Samuelson (Chapter 8) said that the majority of senior economists at Harvard and MIT did not even know the name of the new laureate. His tussle with Keynes had been forgotten as his rival's economic theories were put into practice and further developed by Keynesian economists. However, as we saw in the previous chapter, Keynes's reputation faded in the 1960s and 1970s as it emerged that governments could not control economies as precisely as they had hoped. As a new generation of conservative politicians looked for maps to chart a course away from state control towards free markets, many turned to Friedrich Hayek, who, unlike Adam Smith, was able to see the revival in popularity of his ideas in his own lifetime.

Hayek's legacy can be divided into the purely economic impact of his work, and the way in which it contributed to the political debate, although these are closely connected. His findings in several precise and technical areas – not all of which we have had space to cover in this chapter – are still essential elements in today's economics. We can highlight a small number:

- His idea that over-expansion of credit by central banks as the cause of business cycles finds an echo in modern theories of economic fluctuations.

- The idea that the price system is the way in which individuals with limited knowledge combine to produce one social outcome underpins the rational expectations hypothesis – that people make choices based on their rational outlook, available information and past experiences.

- His thesis that order emerges spontaneously out of apparent chaos is the defining characteristic of the science of complex adaptive systems, which is a key concept in many fields such as biology, financial markets and the study of communities.

- His suggestion that currencies should compete against each other may win new supporters in the wake of the advent of private currencies such as Bitcoins and computer-games-based money.

However, it was Hayek's ideas on the primacy of individuals' decisions over central planning as the best way to run an economy that have had a lasting legacy. When economists started to question the impact that Keynesianism was having on modern economies in the 1960s and 1970s they turned to Hayek. Chief among these new disciples was Milton Friedman, whom we shall meet next (in Chapter 7). He combined Hayek's focus on freedom with his own ideas on how to run the economy into what became known as monetarism. While Hayek himself was not a monetarist as we see them today (he did not believe the money supply could be managed), the emergence of monetarism can be traced back to him.

Although Hayek had left Britain in 1949 it was in the UK that he became best known and where his influence could be most directly felt. Keynesianism suffered its nadir in 1974 when both inflation and unemployment skyrocketed and government intervention appeared powerless to stem either. The following year Margaret Thatcher was elected leader of the Conservative party. Allegedly she had read *Road to Serfdom* while at Oxford University and within months of her accession held a private audience with Hayek at the headquarters of the Institute of Economic Affairs, a free-market think tank.

His influence on her policymaking was clear. According to a famous story, on a visit to the Conservative Research Department she listened to a proposal by one of its staff to find a middle way between the extremes of Left and Right. Before he had finished she pulled a copy of Hayek's *Constitution of Liberty* from her handbag and slammed it down on the table with a cry of 'This is what we believe!' (Careful readers will have observed that Baroness Thatcher's handbag must have been capacious as it was also rumoured to contain *The Wealth of Nations*.)

Once elected in 1979, Margaret Thatcher embarked on a programme that would have plainly appealed to Hayek: cutting the size of the public sector; slashing business red tape; allowing people to buy their council-owned homes; and selling off state-owned industries to citizens. In 1981 she told the House of Commons that she was a 'great admirer' of Professor Hayek and urged 'some' of her fellow MPs to read his works. In a letter to congratulate Hayek on his 90th birthday in 1989, she wrote that the 'leadership and inspiration that your work and thinking gave us were absolutely crucial and we owe you a great deal'.

Across the Atlantic the new US President Ronald Reagan counted both Hayek and Friedman as friends. He too took a leaf out of Hayek's book in devising his election campaign, telling voters that he would 'get the government off our backs [and] out of our pockets'. He took an axe to the federal government and cut taxes – although critics said that his massive increase in defence spending provided a classic Keynesian boost to aggregate demand. In 1991 President George H.W. Bush awarded Hayek the Presidential Medal of Freedom, the country's highest civilian award. 'Future generations will read his works with the same sense of discovery and awe that inspire us today,' the citation read.

While his admirers in the West embraced his defence of liberty as much as his strictures on economic governance, it was in Eastern Europe that Hayek's political philosophy rang loudest. Much of his writing, and *Road to Serfdom* in particular, was based on his experiences of Nazi Germany and his observations of communist Russia (it is said that he only kept references to Russia out of *Road to Serfdom* as he was writing at a time when the Soviets were close allies against Hitler). The collapse of the Soviet Union in the 1980s was a testament to his claims that socialist economies could not work and that the desire for personal liberty was a powerful force – an event he was able to celebrate.

---

*The collapse of the Soviet Union in the 1980s was a testament to Hayek's claims that socialist economies could not work.*

---

*Road to Serfdom* was a strong influence on many of the leaders of the 'velvet' revolution that swept Eastern Europe and culminated in the end of communist rule in Russia itself. Several activists who later become leaders of the newly free countries in Eastern Europe, such as Vaclav Klaus of Poland and Mart Laar of Estonia, have said they were inspired by Hayek. Friedman wrote that Hayek's books were translated and published by the underground and that these black market copies were read widely and undoubtedly influenced the climate of opinion that ultimately brought about the collapse of the Soviet Union.

As we saw (in Chapter 5), the financial crisis and Great Recession of 2008 onwards saw Keynes's thinking come back into the ascendancy as governments rushed to enact stimulus measures to revive demand. In this repeat of the Great Depression scenario, Hayek might have explained the cause of the crisis but would have recommended doing nothing when the banks collapsed. However, as governments pulled back from stimulus and instead focused on cutting the by-now massive public deficits as the best way to restore growth, Hayek's ideas again became popular and actively debated. Around 5 million people have watched 'Fear the Boom and Bust', a rap music debate between Keynes and Hayek, made in 2010, on YouTube. BBC Radio hosted a debate between two leading experts, one on Keynes and one on Hayek, to argue on stimulus versus austerity. As politicians and taxpayers argued over the right course of action to take to deal with the aftermath of the financial crisis, Hayek's thinking would never have been far from their thoughts.

# Verdict: credits and debits

Friedrich Hayek stands out as one of the strongest advocates for personal freedom and opponents of state interference in people's lives. As such he follows in a distinguished line of philosophers such as Adam Smith (see Chapter 1), John Stuart Mill and Edmund Burke. He is still seen as a standard bearer for libertarian movements.

Many economics students study his articles from the 1930s and 1940s on the business cycle, and it would not be surprising if a substantial number of economists were still reading and debating his writings in the year 2092, 100 years after his death. His influence can be felt in current political debates, even if he is not cited by name by advocates of less government interference in the economy.

While Hayek was able to celebrate the fall of communism, his warnings over the pernicious effect on individuals of greater common powers do not often find such a strong echo in modern social democracies, where people tend to accept the mixed economy and welcome state provision of services such as health and education and limits on their freedom such as minimum wages, taxes on pollution and bans on smoking, none of which he would approved of.

# What you should take away

The core tenets of Hayek's writing that are certain to be remembered are:

- Individuals are the root of society and produce social outcomes that no central planner could replicate.

- People in government, however well-intentioned or wise, can never have all the right information to manage a complex system such as the economy.

- The best outcome for society is delivered by allowing individuals to take decisions based on their own fragment of knowledge.

- Attempts to make all people equal – rather than treat them as equal – are a new form of servitude.

# Further reading

Toby Baxendale, *The Battle of the Letters*, The Cobden Centre (2010).

Samuel Brittan, 'F.A. Hayek (1899–1992)', *Oxford Dictionary of National Biography* (Oxford University Press, 2004).

Richard Ebeling, *F.A. Hayek: a biography* (St Martin's Press, 2001).

Alan Ebenstein, *Friedrich Hayek: a biography* (University of Chicago Press, 2003).

Edward Feser (ed.), *The Cambridge Companion to Hayek* (Cambridge University Press, 2006).

Stephen Frowen (ed.), *Hayek: economist and social philosopher* (Palgrave Macmillan, 1997).

Friedrich Hayek, *The Road to Serfdom* (1944).

Friedrich Hayek, *Hayek on Hayek* (1994).

# CHAPTER 7

# Milton Friedman – father of monetarism

'There is no alternative way, so far discovered,
of improving the lot of the ordinary people that can hold
a candle to the productive activities that are unleashed by
a free enterprise system.'
*Milton Friedman, TV interview with Phil Donahue, 1979*

If Keynes wins the award for the finest economist of the first half of the 20th century, then Milton Friedman must surely be in the running for the title for the second half. Like Hayek he made some of his most significant contributions to the wider political debate as well as to the development of modern macroeconomics by arguing that Keynes was wrong. Out of this critique emerged an alternative economic theory that became known in the public arena as 'monetarism'. He is also widely regarded as the leader of the Chicago School of monetary economics, which highlights the importance of the quantity of money as a tool of government policy and as a determinant of business cycles and inflation.

Friedman taught for three decades at the University of Chicago, wrote extensively throughout his life and was one of the first academics to embrace television and the popular press. This meant that he became the first economist to become a genuine household name in America and well-known elsewhere in the world.

Like Hayek, Friedman was interested in the implications of his belief in the free market for personal liberty and how countries should be run as well as in the way it fitted into academic economics. He advised Republican presidents including Richard Nixon and Ronald Reagan. In 1976 he was awarded the Nobel Prize in economics for 'his achievements in the field of consumption analysis, monetary history and theory, and for his demonstration of the complexity of stabilisation policy'.

# Early life and influences

Milton Friedman was born on 31 July 1912 into a fairly typical New York family for the early 20th century. His parents were first-generation Jewish immigrants who had come from what was then Austria-Hungary in a town called Berehove in what is now western Ukraine. He was born in Brooklyn but the family moved to New Jersey while he was still a toddler. His mother ran a small retail 'dry goods' store, while his father engaged in what Friedman junior later described as 'a succession of mostly unsuccessful jobbing ventures' until his premature death aged 49 when his son was 15. Milton Friedman's academic qualities emerged early on, graduating from high school just before he was 16 and earning his first degree aged 20.

Friedman – like Keynes and Marshall – might never have been an economist and instead pursued a career in mathematics. That was the subject that he studied as an undergraduate at Rutgers University and he almost ended his academic career in 1932 to become an actuary. However, he was persuaded by one of the leading economists of the time who happened to be at Rutgers, Arthur F. Burns (later chairman of the US Federal Reserve), to take up a scholarship and embark on a graduate economics degree at the University of Chicago, rather than take an alternative offer to study maths at Brown University.

This decision was to have a profound impact on his life. He met his future wife, fellow economist Rose Director, while on the course – courtesy of the alphabetical seating arrangement in an economics course they both took – and Chicago was to become his spiritual home and the place where he would develop the free-market doctrine for which Chicago is known to this day. In his biography submitted to the Nobel Committee that awarded him the 1976 economics prize, he said: '[Chicago] opened new worlds. It exposed me to a cosmopolitan and vibrant intellectual atmosphere of a kind that I had never dreamed existed. I have never recovered.'

Friedman's early thinking on economics was heavily influenced by the Great Depression. On a personal level he found himself unemployed after leaving Chicago and went to work for the National Resources Committee in Washington, DC – one of the bodies set up by President Franklin D. Roosevelt in the wake of the Great Depression – where he helped construct a large consumer budget study. 'Ironically, the New Deal was a lifesaver for us personally,' Milton and Rose Friedman wrote in their joint memoir, *Two Lucky People*. But his analysis of the Depression led to him coming up with a diagnosis and solution for running economies that was diametrically opposed to that of Keynes and his intellectual disciples.

# The permanent income hypothesis

Friedman's contribution to economics began, not with the high-minded world of finance ministers and central banks, but in the milieu of doctors and dentists. After his work on the New Deal, Friedman got a job at the National Bureau of Economic Research, where he assisted Simon Kuznets – who later won the Nobel for his work on the idea of gross national product – in his studies of professional income.

They concluded that the medical profession's monopoly powers had raised substantially the incomes of doctors relative to those of dentists – indeed, publication of the work, that was completed in 1940, was delayed until after the Second World War because of the controversy it created within the bureau. More important scientifically, the book introduced the concepts of permanent and transitory income. Permanent income broadly translates as the income someone can expect to earn in their lifetime, and transitory income is a windfall.

Friedman combined his findings on professional incomes with the work on consumer spending he had done at the NRC to develop the permanent income hypothesis. The core concept is that people have a good idea of what their income is likely to be on average over the long term. They will then attempt to smooth out their spending over their lifetime by saving some of the extra money they received in the good times to help maintain spending in the bad times (the idea known to economists as 'consumption smoothing' and to prudent households as 'saving for a rainy day').

---

*People have a good idea of what their income is likely to be on average over the long term.*

---

This was Friedman's opening gambit in his bid to dismantle Keynes's analysis of how to resolve economic problems. A Keynesian would say that if people save more in good times, the ratio of spending to income falls as income rises. The idea that people would spend a certain fraction of every extra pound they receive – what Keynes called the propensity to consume – underpinned his idea that cuts in consumer spending caused downturns, and so boosting incomes could help reflate the economy.

Friedman's theory would seek to pull away a key plank of Keynes's analysis: he showed that spending falls much less than

incomes in a downturn because people spend on the basis of
their permanent income rather than any falls in their transitory
incomes. Friedman said therefore that the Depression was
not caused by excess savings; instead he looked for a new
explanation.

# A new explanation for the Great Depression

Friedman's next step was to provide a wholly new explanation
of what caused the Great Depression. He wanted to push back
the idea that it was the result of an excessive upswing in the
business cycle fuelled by excess in the capitalist system and
greedy speculation by unscrupulous investors.

In 1948, together with a colleague, Anna Schwartz, he
looked at the role that the money supply plays in the behaviour
of the economy. They worked for seven years and collected
data on currency and deposits going back to the American Civil
War. It was only after they published their findings in 1963 in *A
Monetary History of the United States* that showed the importance of the money supply that the US Federal Reserve began
tracking money indicators such as M1 (currency plus instant
access deposits) and M2 (M1 plus notice deposit) that they had
developed in their book.

Friedman and Schwartz put the blame for the Great
Depression not on the behaviour of the private sector but on
the 'inept ... mismanagement' of monetary policy by the central
bank. Friedman found that the Federal Reserve allowed the
money supply to contract by 7 per cent, 17 per cent and 12
per cent in 1931, 1932 and 1933 respectively. The Fed actually

*raised* interest rates – to stem a flow of gold from the US after Britain left the gold standard – rather than flood the system with liquid cash, which it did not do until late 1932. The cause of the Great Depression was what Friedman called the Great Contraction.

# Money, monetarism and monetary policy

If a collapse in the money supply was a cause of the Great Depression and the failure to deal with that made things even worse, this begged the question about how important the money supply was in the running of the economy. In a 2004 symposium held to celebrate the 40th anniversary of *A Monetary History*, Friedman said simply that the lesson from that work was 'money does matter'.

He launched the next phase of his counter-revolution against Keynesianism in 1956 with a book called *A Quantity Theory of Money – a restatement*. This theory was not new. It says that the amount of money in the economy multiplied by the velocity (speed) at which it circulates equals prices multiplied by the number of sales (or transactions) of goods. It is expressed as MV = PT. Keynes believed that the velocity of money was highly unstable and when it slowed very sharply it would lead to a liquidity trap (see Chapter 5).

Friedman insisted that the velocity of money was relatively stable and therefore the factor that was likely to change the prices side of the equation was the stock of money in the economy. If governments increase the supply of money, that will lead to inflation. This is why he believed that would have been the right action in the Great Depression but also why he believed central banks should keep a tight rein on the money supply in normal times to prevent an inflationary spike. He famously summarised this by saying: 'Substantial inflation is always and everywhere a monetary phenomenon.'

While Friedman rejected the idea that the government could have a role in controlling the economy through spending and taxation, he did believe it had a major role to play in controlling the money supply. The government should be the monopoly provider of what economists call a 'fiat' currency. Based on the Latin for 'let it be', fiat money is created by the government and neither has any intrinsic value nor is tied to gold. Friedman was certainly no anarchist!

Clearly governments that can print money can stoke inflation and Friedman therefore set out hard and fast rules for central banks to follow. He believed that a stable monetary framework was, as he said in *Capitalism and Freedom*, the 'essential prerequisite' for the effective running of a private-sector market economy. He therefore set out what became known as the 'monetarist rule' that the money supply be increased at a fixed rate every year to keep up with real growth in output and populations. While he changed his mind over that rate of growth, by 1984 he had settled on an increase of 1–3 per cent a year. He believed that government budgets should be balanced over time as Keynesian fiscal expansions were faulty not just because they did not work but because they could not be sustained.

# 'Natural' rate of unemployment

One of Friedman's most lasting contributions that straddled both academia and public policymaking was his work on unemployment. As a monetarist he believed that unemployment would rise and fall during business cycles and that wages would rise and fall as workers and firms found a new equilibrium in the labour market. But what was this equilibrium point?

Friedman developed the idea of a 'natural' rate of unemployment. He said that unemployment would fall to a point where any extra effort to push it lower would simply result in higher inflation. As a result his idea acquired the rather wordy title of the non-accelerating inflation of unemployment or NAIRU (which at least has the advantage of being an acronym that can be pronounced – nay-roo).

While Keynesians believed that there was a trade-off between unemployment and inflation, which allowed well-meaning governments to fine-tune policy by cutting or raising taxes or spending to either control inflation at the cost of more unemployment or vice versa, Friedman believed this distorted the ability of the economy to find its own 'natural rate'.

Friedman warned these interventions could not be sustained and in fact would lead to long-term problems that governments would then struggle to reverse. For example, if a government stimulates the economy and brings down unemployment at the cost of higher prices, workers start to anticipate this. Seeing that prices will, or are likely to, rise they will simply demand higher wages that will in turn lead to higher inflation and so on. Rather than there being a stable relationship between unemployment and inflation, it is an unstable link.

In the long run inflation will have no impact on unemployment because people will factor future inflation into their thinking. Instead unemployment will settle at a 'natural' rate as people adjust to higher inflation.

> *In the long run inflation will have no impact on unemployment.*

This argument, which was also being developed by future fellow Nobel laureate Edmund Phelps, received a huge boost from the 'stagflation' episode of the 1970s when unemployment and inflation both rose despite government attempts to intervene. This graph (Figure 7.1), which Friedman used in his 1976 Nobel acceptance lecture, clearly shows what happened. He plotted the rates of inflation and unemployment in seven

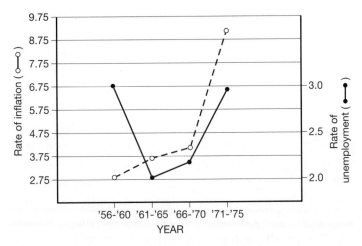

**Figure 7.1   Rates of unemployment and inflation, 1956 to 1975**
*Source*: Friedman, M., 'Inflation and Unemployment', *Journal of Political Economy*, 85, pp. 451–72 (University of Chicago Press, 1977)

industrialised countries over the previous two decades (the G7 minus Canada but including Sweden).

Friedman set out the factors that helped determine the NAIRU. These included 'frictional unemployment' – the fact that people were out of work as they changed jobs or looked for work. He also saw that in some economies workers might have skills that were no longer needed and lacked those that were. Britain saw this 'structural' unemployment in the 1980s when the mass closure of factories during Margaret Thatcher's anti-inflationary policies threw onto the dole large numbers of people who could not find work in the service industries that were taking their place. Friedman included demographic changes such as women joining the workplace or younger workers entering the workforce.

In other words the NAIRU is not a fixed number but something that shifts in line with other changes in the labour market. To bring down that rate, governments should look to improve the way the labour market works, such as providing extra training – what economists call supply side responses – rather than using fiscal or monetary policy to push employment up.

# Advocate of the free market

Like Hayek before him, Friedman became more interested in the wider philosophical and political implications of his theories on the economy. He believed that as well as guiding efficient economic outcomes, individual liberty was also the cornerstone of how societies should operate. He believed that government intervention not only delivered inferior economic outputs, it also made people less well off as human beings because of the coercion involved in using public policy to change behaviours.

But, as mentioned earlier, Friedman did not believe in anarchism (unlike his son David, a market anarchist). He saw a limited role for the state not dissimilar to Adam Smith's duties of the sovereign. Both believed that the state should provide national defence against invasion, establish the legal rules so that markets could work, and control the domestic legal and policing regimes to make sure those rules could be enforced. They also saw that the state should provide some public goods that the market could not provide but which were used by all, such as roads and good education.

But where government went further than that, Friedman saw only tyranny. He warned that when a government got involved in the economy it was likely to act in the interests of the people who controlled or operated the system. This meant that power shifted away from the millions of individuals in society towards those in charge or those who could influence them. Furthermore, someone who cannot, for example, travel to a foreign country, buy or sell particular goods or join a particular profession loses his or her political as well as economic freedom.

Friedman went a step further, saying that more powerful governments would be less likely to allow free expression because raising new ideas and getting them printed or distributed would involve access to funds and permissions that officials in a government would be unlikely to allow if they disagreed with them. By contrast a free-market economy will allow the publication of radical views because a broadcaster or publisher will only be interested in the colour of the writer's money rather than the shade of their political views.

Friedman therefore believed there was a need to limit the role and scope of government, keeping the amount it raises in tax and spend to a minimum. He set out his thinking in three books that span a couple of decades: *Capitalism and Freedom* in 1962; *Free to Choose* in 1980; and *Tyranny of the Status Quo* in 1984, the last two written jointly with his wife.

> *Friedman believed there was a need to limit the role and scope of government.*

Friedman's strong belief in individualism led to him holding beliefs that at first glance you might not expect someone to the right of centre politically to hold. He was against discrimination on grounds of being gay, for example, because such prejudice was an arbitrary judgement that restricted that person's ability to take part in the market as an individual. He also believed that the prejudiced person was imposing a cost on himself – or herself. He supported the libertarian ideals of legalising drugs and prostitution. He also campaigned against military conscription in the United States. Finally he put forward the idea of a negative income tax so that people earning below a certain level would receive money from the state while those earning more would pay higher tax.

# Long-term legacy

Milton Friedman has had a huge influence on the development of economic theory, on the application of monetarism as an economic policy, and on the outlook of many major politicians. He emerged as an economic political thinker at exactly the right time. His writing and theories on economics chimed with a growing disillusionment with the result of the

Keynesianism that many governments had tried to follow. Meanwhile the fall of the Berlin Wall and the collapse of the Soviet Union meant that his and his wife's writing on the political aspects of individualism received attention on both sides of the Iron Curtain.

He certainly helped himself in this regard. Between 1966 and 1983, Friedman wrote a regular column on current affairs for *Newsweek* magazine. But it was *Free to Choose* that cemented his name in the public's mind. The book's first edition sold 400,000 copies but paperback and foreign language editions – there were almost 20 – sold several million and he became as well known in former Soviet states such as Estonia as he was in his native country.

However, it was the television series of the same name, which Friedman made with his wife as associate producer, that catapulted him into millions of living rooms in America and beyond. The programmes consisted of a half-hour presentation by Friedman of a particular economic theme followed by a 30-minute discussion with the 'great and the good' of the era. One biographer, Lanny Ebenstein, said it was 'not too much to say that *Free to Choose* provided much of the domestic blueprint' for Ronald Reagan's presidency. When Friedman first met Queen Elizabeth II, she said her husband, Prince Philip, watched the programme avidly and agreed with every word.

## Economic theory

In terms of economic theory, Friedman's theories permeate modern textbooks: the permanent income hypothesis and the idea of consumption smoothing; the relationship between money, prices and output; the extension of the quantity theory of money; and the natural rate of unemployment, to name a few. But his longstanding contribution in terms of the intellectual journey of economics was to challenge the dominant Keynesian theories and practice in the post-war period and to set out the idea of monetarism.

Without his writing there would not have been the intense intellectual arguments that helped produce the current theories of New Classical Economics and New Keynesianism, and his explanation for the causes of the Great Depression and the way they should have been tackled is now the consensus view of economists. In 2002, before he became chairman of the Federal Reserve, Ben Bernanke apologised for the Fed's role in the Great Depression and addressed the late Milton Friedman directly: 'We're very sorry but thanks to you we won't do it again.'

J.K. Galbraith wrote in his 1987 book *Economics in Perspective* that 'in the history of economics, the age of John Maynard Keynes gave way to the age of Milton Friedman'. One telling indicator of the impact Friedman had on economic doctrine is how Paul Samuelson, the Nobel Prize-winning economist whom we shall meet in the next chapter, subtly changed his interpretation of the significance of monetarism between new editions of his major work, *Economics*. In the 1955 edition Samuelson wrote that 'few economists regard Federal Reserve monetary policy as a panacea for controlling the business cycle'. Almost two decades later in 1973 he said that 'both fiscal and monetary policies matter much' and another two decades later concluded that fiscal policy was 'no longer the tool of stabilisation policy in the US. Over the foreseeable future, stabilisation policy will be performed by Federal Reserve monetary policy.'

Some of the theories that Friedman set out have become part of mainstream economic thinking – whether people agree with them or not. The permanent income hypothesis is one of those, as it is seen as the best way for economists to think about spending and saving patterns among households. The NAIRU has been used as a tool for guiding the setting of interest rates by central banks over the last few decades.

The significant role and power that the Chicago School of economics has in the current macroeconomic debate can be traced back to the amount of effort Friedman put in to establishing the monetarist doctrine at the University of Chicago. In late 2013 two more economists from the university, Eugene Fama and Lars Peter Hansen, who had carried out separate research into the behaviour of asset prices in a way that followed Friedman's logic, won the Nobel Prize.

## Economics in action

The application of Friedman's theories in economic policy has had a mixed track record. As hinted at earlier, Friedman's thinking had a huge influence on the first administrations of both Ronald Reagan in the US and Margaret Thatcher in the UK. Reagan swept to power on a manifesto to control growth in government spending, reform regulations, cut personal income taxes and establish sound and predictable monetary policy. As the Friedmans later wrote in *Two Lucky People*: 'Once in office, Reagan acted very much along the lines we recommended.' Friedman and many economists who cited him as an influence served on the President's Economic Policy Advisory Board.

Across the Atlantic, Margaret Thatcher embraced the policy suggestions set out by Friedman as warmly as she had welcomed F.A. Hayek's vision. Friedman's platform for his views in the UK was the Institute of Economic Affairs (as it had been for Hayek), which published his 1970 lecture 'The Counter-Revolution in Monetary Theory' in which he set out his critique of Keynesianism. It was the IEA that arranged a dinner between Friedman and the then leader of the opposition in 1978.

Friedman has been credited – or blamed, depending on your perspective – for influencing policy in other countries outside the English-speaking world. Most controversial is Chile. Friedman travelled to Chile in 1975, when he met General Augusto Pinochet, who two years earlier had been part of a military coup that overthrew the elected government of President Salvador Allende. Pinochet asked for advice on restoring economic order. In a follow-up letter Friedman said that the only solution to rampaging inflation was 'shock treatment'. Although he repeatedly disavowed the Pinochet junta, the association led to him being barracked by hostile protesters when he spoke abroad. It culminated in public protests at his Nobel Prize award ceremony.

---

*A majority of governments in the West have abandoned fiscal fine-tuning.*

---

A majority of governments in the West have abandoned fiscal fine-tuning and have instead decided to leave that job to central banks, who now target inflation and use interest rates to control the level of economic activity. The Bank of England, the Federal Reserve and the European Central Bank have all run inflation-targeting regimes over the last couple of decades.

The idea of using fiscal policy to fine-tune the economy now receives little support.

But perhaps the greatest endorsement of Friedman's work was the adoption by the Federal Reserve of the medicine he had retrospectively prescribed for the Great Depression, which was vigorously applied in 2009 when central banks slashed interest rates to zero and embarked on 'quantitative easing' – pumping money into the economy.

Giving testimony to the US Congress in that year, Ben Bernanke specifically referenced Friedman and Schwartz's analysis of the Great Depression. 'With that lesson in mind, the Federal Reserve has reacted very aggressively to cut interest rates in this current crisis. Moreover we've tried to avoid the collapse of the banking system.'

On the other hand, disciples of Friedman said the man himself would not have countenanced specific bank and company bailouts that Bernanke and Obama oversaw – as bad banks should be allowed to fail – and would have preferred a larger and more general injection of liquidity. One of those was Schwartz, who said that the Fed was 'fighting the last war' rather than facing up to the need to deal with bad assets.[1]

However, attempts to apply Friedman's monetarist rules in more normal times ran into problems. In his biography of Freidman, economist Eamonn Butler notes that in the periods 1953–57 and 1971–75, US money supply grew at a consistent rate of 2 per cent and 7 per cent a year respectively yet was accompanied by a large amount of economic instability.

---

1. A. Schwartz, 'Bernanke is fighting the last war', *Wall Street Journal*, 18 October 2008.

Attempts to follow particular measures of the money supply in the UK in the 1980s ended after it was shown that direct and predictable links between the growth of the money supply and the rate of inflation broke down. This form of monetarism was replaced first by exchange rate targeting and then by inflation targeting.

Some of Friedman's unorthodox libertarian policy proposals – such as school vouchers and a volunteer army – have gained mainstream acceptance while versions of a negative income tax have found a home in the UK's Working Tax Credit and the US Earned Income Tax Credit. Others, such as the legalisation of drugs and prostitution, may be ideas whose time is yet to come.

# Verdict: credits and debits

Friedman vies for the title of the most influential economist of the late 20th century (probably with Samuelson). Not all his ideas have stood the test of time and few mainstream politicians embrace his thoughts and writing as Reagan and Thatcher did three decades ago. But Friedman-ism is clearly embedded in the new economic consensus. The dominant New Keynesian models that attempted to bring together the best of Keynes and Friedman include the idea of consumption smoothing over time, a primacy of monetary policy and rules for its conduct. Even the policies of quantitative easing that central banks have used since the 2008–9 financial crisis were something Friedman had prescribed to solve Japan's ills 20 years previously.

But despite that achievement it is also clear that few economies have embraced the small government, regulation-lite, purely market economies that Friedman believed in.

Even in his homeland, the public sector takes up as large a percentage of the economy as it did 30 years ago and there is a general acceptance of the need for government regulation to curb the excesses of the free market. Friedman will live on in the teaching and writing about economics even as his personal impact on the public policy debate fades.

# Further reading

Eamonn Butler, *Milton Friedman,* Adam Smith Institute (1985).

Lanny Ebenstein, *Milton Friedman: a biography* (Palgrave Macmillan, 2009).

Milton Friedman, *Studies in the Quantity Theory of Money* (1956).

Milton Friedman, *A Theory of the Consumption Function* (1957).

Milton Friedman, *Capitalism and Freedom* (1962).

Milton Friedman and Anna Jacobson Schwarz, *A Monetary History of the United States, 1867–1960* (Princeton University Press, 1971).

Milton and Rose Friedman, *Free to Choose: a personal statement* (Thomson Learning, 1980).

Milton and Rose Friedman, *The Tyranny of the Status Quo,* new edn (Penguin, 1985).

Abraham Hirsch and Neil de Marchi, *Milton Friedman* (University of Michigan Press, 1991).

William Ruger, *Milton Friedman* (Continuum, 2011).

# CHAPTER 8

# Paul Samuelson – the neoclassical synthesist

'I don't care who writes a nation's laws – or crafts its advanced
treaties – if I can write its economics textbooks.'
*Paul Samuelson, Foreword to* The Principles of Economics
Course: A Handbook for Instructors, *1990*

In the official speech awarding the Nobel Prize in economic
sciences to Paul Samuelson in 1970, Professor Assar Lindbeck,
of the Stockholm School of Economics, said that more than
any other contemporary economist, the new laureate had
contributed to raising the general analytical and methodological
level in economic science. 'He has in fact simply rewritten
considerable parts of economic theory,' he said.

Samuelson's longstanding contribution to economic theory
and practice rests primarily, but certainly not exclusively, on
two specific books out of the hundreds he wrote over a
seven-decade career. His major work, called *Economics: An
Introductory Analysis* and known simply as *Economics*, is
probably the best-selling textbook of all time, selling hundreds
of thousands of copies, reprinted in 19 editions and translated
into 41 languages. But it is his earlier work, *Foundations of
Economic Analysis*, which is considered his magnum opus
because of its role in spreading the revolution of mathematics
in economics.

Samuelson was a self-confessed generalist economist[1] but
made lasting contributions in many fields of the subject such
as consumer theory, welfare economics, international trade,
and to theories of capital and finance and macroeconomics. He
was also central to efforts to put Keynesian economics in a new

---

1. 'In this age of specialisation, I sometimes think of myself as the last
"generalist" in economics' http://www.nobelprize.org/nobel_prizes/
economic-sciences/laureates/1970/samuelson-bio.html

setting and to merge that doctrine with classical economics to produce the then new field of neoclassical economics. He died on 13 December 2009 at the age of 94.


# Early life and influences

Paul Samuelson was born in 1915 in the then booming steel town of Gary, Indiana, in the United States to Jewish immigrants from Poland. His family moved to Chicago in 1923 after his father lost much of his money in the years after the First World War. The cloud created by this enforced move had a silver lining. After shining at high school he went to the University of Chicago at the age of 16. 'I was reborn, born as an economist, at 8.30am on January 2nd 1932, in the University of Chicago classroom,' he said in a memoir published just before his death.[2] The trigger was a lecture about Thomas Malthus, the 18th-century British economist who wrote about population and poverty. From then on Samuelson was hooked on economics.

He graduated with a master's economics degree in 1935 so his time at Chicago coincided with the worst years of the Great Depression. Chicago was already emerged as a haven for neoclassical economists under the influence of Milton Friedman. Samuelson left Chicago to go to Harvard, which was emerging as a bastion of Keynesianism, to study for a doctorate and write his first book, *Foundations of Economic Analysis*, the first draft of which won him the university's David A. Wells

---

2. 'An Interview with Paul A. Samuelson', in Paul Samuelson and William Barnett, *Inside the Economist's Mind* (Wiley/Blackwell, 2007).

Prize in 1941. The book shows that he was clearly unhappy with the arguments used by the classical economists and in particular at their failure to use mathematics.

He specifically targeted Alfred Marshall (see Chapter 4) for what he called 'laborious literary over-workings' of simple mathematical concepts that involve 'mental gymnastics of a peculiarly depraved type'. While this may be unfair on Marshall – who was, as we saw (in Chapter 4), a trained mathematician himself but who believed maths was a limited tool to explain economics – it was a clear sign that Samuelson was keen to use maths to gain a greater understanding of the economic issues of his time. By applying the rigours of maths to economics Samuelson believed he could identify 'striking formal similarities' in areas such as production, consumer behaviour, international trade, public finance, business cycles and the analysis of income.

---

*Samuelson was keen to use maths to gain a greater understanding of the economic issues of his time.*

---

In 1947 and aged just 32 the American Economic Association awarded him the first John Bates Clark Medal as the living American economist under 40 'who has made the most distinguished contribution to the main body of economic thought and knowledge'. In the same year he became a fully-fledged professor at the Massachusetts Institute of Technology (MIT), where he spent the rest of his career. While other economists in this book have been philosophers, speculators or government advisers, Samuelson was first and foremost an educator.

# Key economic theories and writings

Samuelson was an increasingly prolific academic economist, producing an immense volume of audiovisual material, correspondence, magazine articles, research articles, speeches and interviews, teaching material and books, as well as a host of unpublished writings. Through these he developed many of the theorems for which he is still known.

## Paperback writer

A year after receiving his Harvard accolade, Samuelson published *Economics: An Introductory Analysis.* This became the dominant textbook for economics students for the next few decades and as such justifies the view expressed by Samuelson in the quotation at the opening of this chapter. After John Maynard Keynes's (see Chapter 5) death in 1946, Samuelson wrote a glowing eulogy of him in which he said that the Great Depression had made classical economics 'untenable'. 'Instead of burning out like a fad, today 10 years after its birth the *General Theory* is still gaining adherents and appears to be in business to stay,' he wrote.[3]

It was no surprise that the first edition of *Economics* put a lot of stress on what co-author William Nordhaus described in the 14th edition in 1992 as 'Model T Keynesian macro'. Samuelson described himself as a 'cafeteria Keynesian' – taking the bits that suited him.[4] Key Keynesian concepts such as the

---

3. P. Samuelson, 'Lord Keynes and the General Theory', *Econometrica*, 14 (1946), 187–99.
4. http://www.theatlantic.com/politics/archive/2009/06/an-interview-with-paul-samuelson-part-one/19572/

fiscal multiplier, the propensity to consume, the paradox of thrift, countercyclical fiscal policy and the concept of GDP being the sum of private spending, government spending and investment took centre stage in the book.

Samuelson said that 'private enterprise' was frequently hit by 'acute and chronic cycles' in unemployment, output and prices, which governments had a duty to 'alleviate'. 'The private economy is not unlike a machine without an effective steering wheel or governor …'. 'Cocompensatory fiscal policy tries to introduce such a governor or thermostatic control device.'

While early editions emphasised the superiority of fiscal policy over monetary policy as the best way to stabilise the economy, this position had been completely reversed by the 15th edition (1995), which said that fiscal policy was no longer a 'major tool of stabilisation policy' in the United States. 'Over the foreseeable future, stabilisation policy will be performed by Federal Reserve monetary policy.'

Despite this shift in emphasis as Samuelson and other economists grappled with the challenge that the inflationary recessions of the 1970s had posed to Keynesian thinking, *Economics* achieved its role of reformulating Keynes's thinking into a college textbook that Keynes's own *General Theory* – with its ornate style and inherent contradictions – could never be. But at the same time Samuelson incorporated the increasingly important monetarist theories that were emerging from Chicago and the other so-called 'freshwater' universities that were focused on free-market economics.

It should not be overlooked that Samuelson also set out the basics of the microeconomic market system – why and how consumers and businesses behave in the way that they do. *Economics* devotes considerable room to explaining how markets function and how they solve the central problems of economics that concerned Adam Smith: what to produce, how to produce it, and for whom to produce it. 'A competitive system of markets and prices – whatever else it may be, however imperfectly it may function – is not a system of chaos and anarchy,' Samuelson wrote. 'There is in it certain order and orderliness. It works.'

Samuelson made contributions across the broad landscape of economics – unlike today, when economists specialise early in their careers and become experts in the minutiae of one particular field. As a generalist – something that Samuelson himself said he could not have been if he had started out any later than the 1940s – he made findings in microeconomics, macroeconomics and in international trade.

## A new home for Keynes

Samuelson used his best-selling textbook as a new home of Keynesian thinking in the post-war period. Along with other economists such as John Hicks and Franco Modigliani, he worked to create the models that would provide a mathematical underpinning to Keynes's ideas. This became known as neo-Keynesianism, and neo-Keynesian economics dominated mainstream macroeconomic thought in the post-war period.

However, the stagflation of the early 1970s and the rising popularity of monetarism cast doubt on the use of policies put forward by Keynesians – neo- or otherwise.

The stagflation episode forced Samuelson and his academic

allies to marry neo-Keynesianism with the microeconomics of the classical economic school. They created the 'neoclassical synthesis' – a term believed to have been coined by Samuelson. This combined the classical emphasis on the ability of markets to self-correct and the role of shocks in triggering business cycles that operated in the good times, while retaining Keynes's thinking on aggregate demand and the role of government in correcting downturns. This theory has played a major role in mainstream economic teaching and policymaking since the 1970s. However, it has been criticised for its failure to foresee the 2007–8 global financial crisis.

Samuelson made a number of improvements to the Keynesian analysis of macroeconomics. He took the multiplier effect that Keynes developed that said that an injection of money into the economy by the government would have a greater impact on the economy than the sum of new money alone in the form of extra wages and spending for new workers taken on. Samuelson said that as economic output expanded then businesses would need to invest in new capital. These factors would feed off each other as the increase in investment led to more output thanks to the multiplier that in turn leads to more investment. In a downturn the multiplier-accelerator effect operates in reverse as cuts in investment leads to falls in output (via the multiplier) that in turn lead to falls in investment (via the accelerator).

Samuelson showed how these could create business cycles using an 'oscillator' model. The amplitude of the variations in economic output depends on the level of the investment, for investment determines the level of aggregate output (multiplier), and is determined by aggregate demand (accelerator). The model showed how markets magnify the impact of outside shocks and turn, say, an initial one-dollar increase in foreign investment into a several-dollar increase in total domestic income.


## Public goods and public finance

While *Economics* is certain to remain Samuelson's lasting monument in the world of economics, he never stopped researching and writing and introduced a host of concepts to the discipline. Within six years of the publication of the first editions of the textbook, Samuelson set out a theory of public goods and the conditions needed to ensure they were efficiently provided.

Samuelson wanted to answer the question of how scarce resources could be allocated efficiently in a world of both private goods and public goods. A public good is one where no one can be excluded from using it, and where one person's use does not make it less available for others. Examples range from lighthouses off dangerous cliffs to public beaches and a national defence system. To give a modern example, the global positioning satellite is available to everyone (subject to buying a GPS device) to enable them to go mountain climbing, long-distance driving, or judge the distance of a golf ball from the hole. One person's use does not diminish anyone else's ability to use it and no one can be prevented from using it.

In his 1954 paper *The Pure Theory of Public Expenditure* – just two pages long but so far cited almost 6,000 times in other academic journals – Samuelson drew a distinction between private consumption goods and public consumption goods. He defined public goods as ones 'all enjoy in common in the sense that each individual's consumption of such a good leads to no subtractions from any other individual's consumption of that good'.[5]

---

*Samuelson drew a distinction between private consumption goods and public consumption goods.*

---

In other words, public goods are those whose consumption by one person does not mean less consumption by anyone else. The features of public goods stand in direct contrast to those of ordinary goods, such as bread. A loaf eaten by one consumer is not available to anyone else. As a result, Samuelson said, there was no 'decentralised' pricing mechanism that would lead the private sector to provide those goods.

The private sector generally does not guarantee efficient production of public goods because it cannot capture the wider benefits of the GPS system or, say, a cure for malaria. For this reason private companies are unlikely to produce that good or service, knowing they will not get rewarded for it.

A similar but reverse analysis applied to public goods such as clean air. Because a factory does not have to pay for polluting the air and so reducing the quality of that public good for everyone else, it will continue to use up that resource. The

---

5. Paul A. Samuelson, 'The Pure Theory of Public Expenditure', *The Review of Economics and Statistics*, Vol. 36(4) (November 1954), pp. 387–9.

pricing system cannot force consumers to reveal their demand for public goods, and so cannot force producers to meet that demand.

Samuelson concluded that public goods could be provided – or protected – effectively only through collective, or government, action because the market would fail to do so. Public goods cannot be bought and sold in private markets because consumers have no incentive to pay for them voluntarily. Instead they hope to get a 'free ride' on others' decisions to make the public goods available.

Samuelson's two-page paper has led to the creation of a standalone discipline of public goods economics that has generated a huge volume of research. His theory has underpinned the way that governments justify decisions to spend money on one activity on the basis that it can only be provided by the state (such as the armed services) or that it can be provided more effectively than by the private sector alone. An example of the latter is healthcare in some countries such as the UK, where the government believes that it can better guarantee the knock-on benefits of good health for employers and taxpayers by providing healthcare.

One of the most fecund areas is the study of global public goods. These include issues as disparate as greenhouse warming and ozone depletion, information on the internet, money laundering, the discovery of antibiotics and nuclear proliferation. Reducing global warming would benefit everyone, not just today but for future generations too. However, cutting harmful emissions would be costly. The accumulation of carbon dioxide in the atmosphere in the two centuries following the Industrial Revolution illustrates Samuelson's theory. The painfully slow efforts by governments to agree on a deal to cut emissions show how difficult it is to overcome the 'free rider' problem. As Samuelson's collaborator William Nordhaus has put it: 'The requirement for unanimity is in reality a recipe for inaction.'[6]

## Intergenerational economics

Another major breakthrough was the overlapping gener-ations (OLG) model that captured the changing behaviour of consumers over different phases of their lives and how those decisions affect the growth of the overall economy. The core idea is that everyone lives through three specific time periods, in the first two of which they work, earn and save money and in the last of which they retire and spend but earn no money.

When people are young they can sell their labour to businesses and then divide their earnings between spending now and saving for old age. Someone in their middle period, looking to secure an income in their third period, realises she must lend someone money – in a real-life example she would look to a pension provider – who will pay her back with interest in the final period of her life. When she retires she will live off the income based on the money she accrued earlier in her life. In the meantime firms produce an output by employing the labour supplied by those young workers, but also by using the capital that has been made available by those workers' savings (such as pension funds taking large shareholdings in businesses).

---

6. W. Nordhaus, 'Paul Samuelson and Global Public Goods: a commem-orative essay for Paul Samuelson' (5 May 2005) http://www.econ.yale.edu/~nordhaus/homepage/PASandGPG.pdf

While Samuelson's theory was purposefully model-based and made assumptions that did not always equate with real life, the framework of the model provided the basis for future research. By modelling savings at an individual level, Samuelson's OLG model opened up another way to examine the impact of various policies on the behaviour of the economy over an indefinite future.

It provided the basis for future research and thinking about intergenerational problems. In particular it underpinned a paper by fellow Nobel laureate Peter Diamond, who added fixed capital and money into the equation, paving the way for applications to issues such as social security.

To help people understand Samuelson's theory one economist, Laurence Kotlikoff, conjured up the image of a hot desert island where the only source of food was chocolate bars hanging at the top of cocoa trees. The young can harvest them but eat them at once (because of the heat) and refuse to give any to their elderly parents because they see no benefit in handing them over. At some point one pensioner gathers seashells off the beach and offers them in exchange for chocolate. The young agree to the deal, realising that by doing so they will accumulate shells that will enable them to buy chocolate in their old age.

These models underpin current debates about the afford-ability of social security systems in western economies, where high levels of consumption and low levels of savings by working households may lead to problems for the increasingly large generation of pensioners. While models used by economists that include demographic change, tax measures and the role of the government in funding care for the elderly have become increasingly complicated, they are ultimately based on the original OLG idea.

Later economists built versions that enabled it to become a staple of macroeconomic models. As fellow Nobel laureate Paul Krugman said after Samuelson's death: '[His] 1958 overlapping-generations model of borrowing and lending is the framework for thinking about everything from social security to household debt. It's hard to imagine macro without it.'[7]

## Understanding consumers

One of the first areas where Samuelson made a significant impact was in the understanding of consumers' behaviour. At that point most models were based on the idea of the marginal rate of substitution – the amount of one good (such as a hamburger) that a consumer is willing to give up for another good (such as a cinema ticket). The weakness in this idea is that it involves making assumptions about the levels of people's enjoyment (or utility, as economists called it). Asking someone to say how much utility she gets from a hamburger or a trip to the cinema will certainly prompt a very baffled expression.

---

*Economists should work out which goods consumers prefer over others.*

---

Instead Samuelson saw that the key was to find a way to actually measure people's preferences by analysing how they behaved. Rather than worrying about the number of goods people said they wanted to buy, economists should work out which goods

---

7. http://www.voxeu.org/article/paul-samuelson-incomparable-economist

consumers prefer over others. The revealed preference theory works backwards from consumers' purchasing decisions to deduce their preferences.

A consumer shows her preferences by the choices she makes – hence the term 'revealed preferences'. By observing the choices that consumers make, given changes in the prices for goods and changes in their personal income situations, one can see which bundles of commodities they prefer. Assuming that consumers then behave in a rational way when faced with these choices will allow economists to construct models of consumer demand. Using our example, one can measure consumers' preference for a hamburger meal or cinema ticket by seeing how many of each they buy as prices change and incomes vary.

While this is a relatively technical area of economics, it has proved to be very important. Rather than requiring economists who want to predict consumer demand to use some notional concept of utility, revealed preference uses only information on the choices consumers make when faced with different prices and income situations while assuming that they make those choices in a rational way. This can help economists predict how consumers behave when their income rises or falls, and when prices rise or fall.

## Welfare economics

Since the time of thinkers such as Adam Smith (see Chapter 1), John Stuart Mill and Jeremy Bentham, economists have sought how to evaluate economic policies in terms of their effects on the wider community's wellbeing. What does it mean to say that one economic outcome is better than another? The classical argument was that social welfare was the sum of individuals' preferences – from which came the concept of utilitarianism, that all action should be directed towards achieving the greatest happiness for the greatest number of people.

When Samuelson came to the topic much of the groundwork had been laid down by the Italian economist Vilfredo Pareto, who introduced the concept now known as Pareto efficiency. This describes the point at which it is impossible to make any one individual better off without making at least one other worse off. In 1938 an economist called Abram Bergson developed the idea of a social welfare function that ranks different states of society as less desirable, more desirable or indifferent when compared with another. Bergson said that had to rest on ethical judgements.

Samuelson's starting point was the position that formed the basis for Bergson's social welfare function: that welfare economics implied making ethical judgements. The crucial step was recognising that the theory of the consumer and the theory of welfare economics needed to be clearly separated, as consumer theory did not in itself have welfare implications, and that welfare economics required the introduction of ethical judgements.

Samuelson constructed what is now known as the Bergson–Samuelson social welfare function. It was based on the idea that economists can include any value judgements, irrespective of whose ethical beliefs they represent, whether or not they are widely shared in the society, or how they are generated in the first place. It aggregates individual utilities or preferences to develop a well-defined set of preferences for society as a whole. While changes in society will make some better off and some worse off, in what Samuelson said was a 'just' society, compensation payments would be made to maximise the collective social welfare. Although the theory has been overtaken by other economists, it provided the basis for the introduction of ethics into economics. It shows how to represent all real-valued economic measures of any belief system that is required to rank consistently different feasible social configurations in an ethical sense as 'better than', 'worse than', or 'indifferent to' each other.

Samuelson then extended this to look at how families made welfare decisions. He first put forward the idea of looking at how families behaved by studying what each member of the family would choose and how they would then come up with a consensus view of the way in which they could best maximise the family's utility (rather than assume there was a family utility).

Where Samuelson focused on a family's demand for goods and supply of labour, the economics of the family now takes as its domain a wide spectrum of family behaviours: household production, the allocation of time and goods within the family, marriage, divorce, fertility, investment in children's human capital and care of disabled family members. We will examine these issues in more detail in the chapter on Gary Becker.

## International economics and trade

The economics of international trade occupied Samuelson's thinking across the decades during which he was researching and writing. We saw (in Chapter 2) that he selected David Ricardo's doctrine of comparative advantage as one proposition in the social sciences that was both true and non-trivial. He made findings in many key areas of this complex subject that still hold significance today, drawing on his thinking about revealed preference and his welfare analysis.

---

## *What does it mean to say that international trade is beneficial?*

---

Samuelson answered a question that continues to resonate today: what does it mean to say that international trade is beneficial? The starting point is Samuelson's analysis of the gains from trade, which drew on both revealed preference and his welfare analysis. He used revealed preference to show that a country that embraced trade with other countries would enjoy greater welfare than if it closed its borders and lived in what Samuelson called autarky (meaning self-sufficiency, from the ancient Greek words for 'self' and 'to suffice').

He then went a stage further and looked at what would happen when two countries both produced two goods but with different levels of labour and capital (what economists call factors). Working with Austrian-born economist Wolfgang Stolper, he showed that as those countries opened up to trade, the gains would accrue to the sectors that used the relatively abundant factor and the losses to those using scarce ones. So a capital-rich country (such as the US) will see its return on capital rise but wages fall as it trades with, say, China, which would see wages increase but returns on capital fall. While both sides will benefit there will be a split in how those gains and losses are distributed.

Samuelson and Stolper's analysis is essential in understanding why wages are rising in emerging economies and why the manufacturing base is shrinking in western countries. While it was written in 1941, one can see immediately how it shines a light on the current trade imbalances between the West and Asia today.

Of course their finding that exports from labour-rich underdeveloped countries could drive down the wages of low-paid workers in industrialised countries was used as intellectual ammunition by advocates of protectionism. Indeed, late in his career Samuelson showed that a rich country could be harmed if productivity rose among the economies with which it traded. Yet Samuelson, like most academic economists, remained an advocate of free trade. He showed that trade raised average living standards enough to allow the workers and consumers who benefited to compensate those who lost out, and still have some extra income left over.

The Stolper–Samuelson theorem supports the basic prediction of international trade theory that economies will gain overall from tariff reductions and freer trade. But it also highlights the potential for distributional conflict over trade policy. Unless compensation for income losses is actually paid to the losers to ensure that trade remains open, there are always both winners and losers from any change in trade policy. This argument has been played out in every major international negotiation on liberalising global trade right up to the December 2013 summit of the World Trade Organization in Bali.

A connected finding – and one that still has traction today – is the impact that trade has on exchange rates. Fast-growing countries will have strengthening real exchange rates and rich countries will have higher exchange rates than poor countries. The basis is the strong rates of productivity that fast-growing countries tend to see in export industries (such as mass manufacturing) versus non-tradable businesses (such as hairdressing).

Assuming that labour and capital can move between different sectors, the fast-growing export-oriented sector will suck in workers, money and raw material, pushing up wages and prices. But this, in turn, will make production in the non-traded goods more expensive, and bid up prices there. One long-run impact of this thinking was the creation of purchasing price parity (PPP) measures of economic growth used by organisations such as the International Monetary Fund to measure national economies using market domestic exchange rates and national prices rather than expressing growth in dollar terms.

The other major finding that stands out from the many Samuelson made on trade goes by the awkward name of the factor price equalisation theorem. Economists have known for some time that the free movement of capital and labour – as was seen during the British Empire and the mass migration to America – could equalise rates of return between the old and new worlds. But could trade in goods have the same impact?

Samuelson proved that in theory trade between two countries with the same commodity prices and levels of technology would lead to prices of the output goods falling to the same level, which would lead to the prices of the factors of production (capital and labour) also equalising between the two countries.

In reality this does not always happen. Other factors such as migration controls, different levels of technology and differences in the quality of the rule of law between countries mean that prices and wages do not always fall in line (such as can be seen between the US and Mexico within the North American Free Trade Agreement). However, the theory provides a key intellectual underpinning of trade economics.

## Financial economics

Towards the end of his career Samuelson looked at financial economics, which fitted well with the increasing financialisation of economies from the 1980s onwards. He examined two specific areas that, as with trade, welfare economics and overlapping generations, enabled others to subsequently construct more complex edifices – efficient markets and warrant pricing.

The first was Samuelson's discovery that in competitive markets, where participants have full access to information, price movements over time will be essentially random. This influenced the trend among the investor community towards index-based funds rather than striving to achieve superior performance by 'beating' the market. It also laid the foundation of the efficient-market hypothesis, the theory set out by Eugene Fama, who shared the Nobel Prize in 2013 for that work. Similarly his work on the pricing of warrants – options to buy, at a future date, stock issued by a company – laid the ground for research on how to price financial options. This earned Nobel Prizes for Robert Merton, Fischer Black and Myron Scholes, but also led indirectly to the massive growth in complex financial products.

# Long-term legacy

There is no doubt that Paul Samuelson has left a permanent imprint on the understanding and teaching of economics. In a career that spanned seven decades he wrote innumerable papers on a huge number of issues across the broad spectrum of economics. After his death in December 2009 at the age of 94 there was an outpouring of tributes to him, all of which focused on the impact he had had in so many different areas.

This chapter has summarised just a few of the major breakthroughs that he made. While his conclusions and theorems were often not the final word on any particular issue, whether on trade, public finance or consumer behaviour, his findings established the solid foundations on which subsequent economists established new theories.

---

*Samuelson's work transformed how economics was – and still is – taught.*

---

While there are today several textbooks on the principles of economics, Samuelson wrote one of just five books to have stood out in that educational arena over the last 250 years' history of the discipline. *Economics* can be ranked alongside Smith's *Wealth of Nations* (see Chapter 1); Ricardo's *The Principles of Political Economy and Taxation* (Chapter 2); *Principles of Political Economy*, by John Stuart Mill; and Marshall's *Principles of Economics* (Chapter 4). His work transformed how economics was – and still is – taught.

CHAPTER 8 • PAUL SAMUELSON                                    **189**

Looked at from a more recent perspective, Samuelson's *Economics* took Keynes's *General Theory* (Chapter 5) – which was never something that could be used as a student textbook – and injected a degree of simplification and modification that made it palatable for undergraduates. At the same Samuelson incorporated the anti-Keynes positions developed by monetarist economists as they evolved over the course of the 19 editions of the book.


## Economic theories

Samuelson was the last of the great generalist economists, making important contributions on trade, macroeconomics, public finance and consumer behaviour. In particular areas of economies his name continues to resonate. His work on macroeconomics still informs the ongoing debate between neo-Keynesians and neo-monetarists who are seeking to establish a new economic theory in the wake of the financial crisis.

His work on defining a public good and examining how it can be allocated outside the market mechanism still informs a vigorous debate among politicians and economists eager to solve issues such as saving species from extinction and tackling climate change. His work on revealed preferences is central to understanding consumer demand while his overlapping generations model still underpins the increasingly fraught debate over funding ageing populations.

Samuelson's ideas on trade still inform the debate between free traders and protectionists, who can both take ammunition from his wide-ranging research. As Kenneth Rogoff, an economics professor at Harvard University, said in a collection

of essays celebrating Samuelson's work:[8] 'If and when interplan-
etary trade ever commences (say, via radio beam exchanges of
technological blueprints and music), economists of the day will
quickly find themselves trotting out expositions of Samuelson's
1948 paper.'

## Economics in action

While happiest when researching, writing and teaching,
Samuelson did have an impact on the public economic
debate. As the leading post-war Keynesian economist he
was the obvious person for then Senator John F. Kennedy
to pick as his chief economic adviser, a position that he held
right through to the newly elected president's inauguration.
He declined to go to Washington, instead helping to choose
the members of the Council of Economic Advisors and
contributing advice from his office at MIT when required.
After Kennedy's assassination Samuelson continued to advise
President Lyndon B. Johnson. Samuelson's economics now
has its own family lineage: his late brother Robert Summers
(who changed his surname) was a professor at the University
of Pennsylvania, his sister-in-law Anita is an emerita professor
at the same university and his nephew Lawrence Summers
served on President Barack Obama's National Economic
Council until 2010.

Samuelson was a regular columnist for *Newsweek* from
September 1966 to May 1981. He wrote almost 250 of these
columns, for many years in a three-week rotation with Milton

---

8. M. Szenberg, L. Ramrattan and A.A. Gottesman (eds), *Samuelsonian
   Economics and the Twenty-First Century* (Oxford University Press,
   2006).

Friedman and Henry Wallich, a Yale economist and US central banker. Much of that period saw him sparring with Friedman in particular. Although Samuelson said he was nervous of debating directly with Friedman – who was also a close personal friend – he represented the Keynesian tradition of government intervention and regulation against his counterpart's strong free-market views.

# Verdict: credits and debits

Kenneth Arrow, a fellow Nobel laureate economist, said in the introduction to the collection of essays celebrating Samuelson's work that 'modern economics is inconceivable without his accomplishments'. Paul Krugman, another laureate, said Samuelson had 'literally created' at least eight whole fields of economics, any one of which would have earned him a place among history's greatest economic thinkers.

Samuelson's seven-decade career means that he is one of the few economists who spans the Great Depression and the recent global financial crisis. His output therefore acts as a bridge across the economic trends that spanned that period – classical economics, Keynesianism, monetarism, neo-Keynesianism and neoclassical theory.

But that does not tell the full story of his vast contribution to our understanding of economics. He did not have the personal identity that Keynes, Friedman and others in this book do, but without his work it is hard to know where economics would be today. Since the global financial crisis, however, there has been a strong pushback against both the failure of mainstream economics to foresee the crisis and the focus by economists on mathematical proof. Only time will tell what impact that debate will have on Samuelson's long-term reputation.


# Further reading

K. Puttaswamaiah, *Paul Samuelson and the Foundations of Modern Economics* (Transaction Publishers, 2001).

Paul Samuelson, *Foundations of Economic Analysis* (1947).

Paul A. Samuelson, *Economics: an introductory analysis* (1948).

Paul A. Samuelson, *Collected Scientific Papers* (1966).

Paul Samuelson (ed.), *Inside the Economist's Mind* (2007).

Mark Skousen, 'The Perseverance of Paul Samuelson's Economics', *Journal of Economic Perspectives*, Vol. 11(2) (1997), pp. 137–52.

E. Cary Soloki and Robert M. Brown (eds), *Paul Samuelson and Modern Economics Theory* (McGraw-Hill, 1983).

Michael Szenberg, Lall Ramrattan and Aron A. Gottesman (eds), *Samuelsonian Economics and the Twenty-First Century* (Oxford University Press, 2006).

John Cunningham Wood (ed.), *Paul A. Samuelson: critical assessments* (Routledge, 2005).

# CHAPTER 9

# Gary Becker – economics in the real world

'I was not sympathetic to the assumption that criminals had
radically different motivations from everyone else.'
*Gary Becker, Prize Lecture to the memory of Alfred Nobel,*
*9 December 1992*

# Introduction

Many economists have been accused of seeking to solve mathematical equations without thinking about the real-life impact
of their theories. Gary Becker is certainly no slouch in terms of
academic economics, but he has applied a neoclassical view of the
discipline to a range of very 'real world' problems that were previously thought to be the sole domain of sociologists and lawyers.
These included racial discrimination, crime and punishment,
how families work, and understanding drug addiction.

His citation for the 1992 Nobel Prize for economic sciences,
which was awarded to him alone that year, referred to his
work in extending 'the domain of microeconomic analysis to
a wide range of human behaviour and interaction, including
non-market behaviour'. His analysis is rooted in the idea that
human behaviour is rational and that people respond to incentives in a way that maximises their own happiness.

---

*People respond to incentives in a way that*
*maximises their own happiness.*

---

Becker is steeped in the Chicago school of thinking and has
taught at the University of Chicago, where he also completed

his doctorate in 1955, since 1968. In 1967 he won the John Bates Clark Award for the American economist under the age of 40 judged to have made the most significant contribution to economic thought and knowledge. Although his ideas were initially greeted with scepticism, it is now clear he has influenced vast areas of thinking, both within and outside of economics.

# Early life and influences

Gary Stanley Becker was born on 2 December 1930 into the Great Depression era, although he was not personally affected by it. He was the son of a small business owner, Louis Becker, who had moved to Pottsville, a coal-mining town in Pennsylvania after quitting school in Montreal, Canada, at the age of 14 and moving to the US to make money. Becker senior's forebears were Jewish immigrants from Eastern Europe as were those of Becker junior's mother, Anna Siskind, whose family emigrated to New York City when she was six months old. She also left school early, so in a way Becker did not grow up in the fiercely academic atmosphere that some of the others in this book did.

Becker has said that there were not that many books at home although his father kept up with the financial and political news. It might not seem the ideal breeding ground for a future Nobel economist, but with the benefit of hindsight Becker was able to identify some of the factors that might have pushed him in that direction. He went to school in Brooklyn after his family had moved to New York City.

In his biography for the Nobel award Becker said that at the age of 16 he had to choose between being a member of the maths team and of the handball squad, both of which he excelled in. 'It was indicative of my shift in priorities that I chose math, although I was better at handball,' he wrote. He also said that there were many 'lively discussions' in the house about politics and justice. 'I believe this does help explain why by the time I finished high school, my interest in mathematics was beginning to compete with a desire to do something useful for society.'

He went on to take a BA at Princeton University, completing the course in three rather than four years and graduating in 1951 by taking extra courses in advanced mathematics over the summer. He has said he 'accidentally' took a course in economics while at the Ivy League university. He was motivated to study a subject with a social impact and had initially considered sociology but decided the subject was too difficult. He enrolled in the graduate economics programme at Chicago University.

It was here that the die was cast in terms of what areas he would focus on. He graduated in 1955 with a PhD thesis entitled *The Economics of Racial Discrimination*, and said he was profoundly influenced by the microeconomics courses taught by Milton Friedman (Chapter 7). While Friedman gave him a solid grounding in the classical approach to micro-economics, he was also exposed to leading scholars of labour markets, human capital, industrial organisation and on probability and statistics.

His breakthrough moment came in 1957 after he had taken a post at Columbia University, when he published a book based on his PhD thesis and entitled *The Economics of Discrimination*. This set out to recast discrimination within an economic context by using algebra to represent how the discrimination exercised by employers, employees and consumers added to the costs that they weighed up when deciding to go ahead with an agreement to hire, take on a job or buy a good or service. Becker was set on a career examining how economics could explain and alleviate the social issues that were then bedevilling the US economy.

# Key economic theories and writings

Becker believed that the ways that humans behaved in making economic decisions were determined by a fundamental set of economic principles. Behind these was the belief that individuals, whether people, firms or governments, tended to behave in a rational way and to pursue the course that gave them the greatest increase in their welfare. He applied these ideas to areas where scientists had previously assumed that behaviour was formed by entrenched habits or was simply irrational and thus not open to logical explanation.

It is important to stress that this assumption about rational behaviour was more than simply adopting the doctrine of enlightened self-interest put forward by Adam Smith (Chapter 1). Becker also saw that individuals were motivated by more than simply selfishness or gain, as Marx believed (Chapter 3). Instead they were motivated to pursue their greater personal benefit, but one that economists should see as coming from a richer set of values and preferences.

# Discriminating against minorities

This area was not only the first that Becker tackled – initially
in his doctoral thesis – but also the one that helped define
how he approached economic issues. He recalls that the
book he published while at Chicago provoked a couple of
positive reviews but little mainstream interest. Indeed many
fellow economists considered that it was not really economics.
However, he said that the support he received from Friedman
and other professors at Chicago gave him the resilience to carry
on in that field.

When Becker started out as an economist there was little
literature about discrimination and nothing from an economic
perspective. Adam Smith had understood that different jobs
would be paid more if they were unpleasant or difficult but
he had not looked at how that might be affected by people's
views. Becker started out by seeing how economic theory could
explain why people discriminated against blacks in particular
but also against other racial minorities and against women, and
how that fed into the economic system.

*Discrimination has a monetary impact.*

Clearly discrimination has a monetary impact. If a black person
with the same skills as a white candidate always loses out for
the job and instead has to take work at a lower level he will
clearly earn less over time. If blacks find it harder to get work
there will be higher levels of unemployment, which again has
a financial cost. But how can an economist identify the factors
that lead to those decisions?

Becker abandoned the typical assumptions that employers only considered the productivity of potential employees; that workers ignored the characteristics of those that they worked for; and that customers only cared about the qualities of the goods and services provided. He devised 'discrimination coefficients' that incorporated the impact of race, gender and other personal characteristics on tastes and attitudes.

At its core the analysis is based on the idea that people mentally account for a cost – albeit a non-monetary one – when they do business with someone against whom they hold a prejudice. The immediate cost falls on the minority individual, whether as a potential employee, employer or retailer as they bear the cost of prejudice. This is especially so when the victims of discrimination are in the minority. However, Becker highlighted an important new aspect – that the person who discriminates also loses as they almost certainly miss out on a valuable opportunity that they ignored through prejudice.

However, when the victims are in the majority the costs more obviously fall on both sides as, for example, an employer who closes his mind to the majority of potential applicants is unlikely to get the best candidates. Becker himself saw this as one of the explanations for the eventual collapse of apartheid in South Africa where that majority/minority scenario was most clearly in operation.

Becker saw that competition would be the vital ingredient in eliminating discrimination, as employers who took on the workers that others shunned would gain a competitive advantage. He also presented evidence that discrimination is more pervasive in more-regulated, and therefore less-competitive, industries.

# Building human capital

It may be an irksome phrase beloved of management consultants, but back in the 1950s few had heard of the concept of human capital until Becker developed the theory and wrote a best-selling book of the same name. Up until then economists believed that people's labour power was given. Becker decided to look at how investment in people's education and training paid off.

He said that the investment into someone's knowledge in the form of better education and higher skills was as much an asset as stocks and shares, buildings, machinery and technology. What both had in common was the potential to deliver a long-term income stream and to act as a catalyst for growth elsewhere in the economy.

Becker has said this idea ran into hostility from people who saw it as demeaning to treat people in the same way as machines. But his view – groundbreaking at the time – was that schooling, on-the-job training, medical care and acquiring general and specific knowledge were all forms of investment. But unlike physical capital they could not be separated from their owners.

He started out with an attempt to build an empirical understanding of how much people would benefit in terms of their earnings by going to university rather than leaving education after secondary school and what happened to their employment – and unemployment – opportunities over their careers. He then looked at how people weighed the costs and benefits of improving their education, knowledge, training and skills.

From this Becker built a general theory of human capital that included firms as well as individuals and specified the relation between earnings and human capital that could be used in terms of its macro-economic implications. Improving the supply side of the economy – the quality of the way that the economy operates – can increase the potential long-term output of an economy in a different way from trying to boost demand.

Economists such as the Harvard academic Richard Freeman and Becker's fellow Chicagoan Kevin Murphy have shown how the declines in the benefits of university education in the US in the 1970s and the subsequent rebound to high levels (in terms of differences in average earnings between university graduates and school leavers) correlate with the numbers of new enrolments.

Becker used the economic concept of opportunity cost to show how students saw that the cost of taking a university education was not just the up-front fees but also the greater cost of staying out of the labour market and losing earnings for three or more years. This shows that in periods of recession or low growth, when earnings tend to rise nominally if at all, it makes economic sense to give up those wages and invest in a better education that should pay dividends in the long run. Inherent in this is the idea of time as a cost: impatient people will invest less in their own human capital because they cannot bear to wait to reap the benefits of the investment.

Becker also distinguished between general and specific training/knowledge, with the latter important in a particular firm but the former useful to all employers. The distinction helps explain why workers with very specific skills are likely to receive higher salaries to prevent them leaving and why they tend to be the last to be made redundant during economic downturns. It also explains why most firms make promotions from within the organisation rather than through hiring, as new workers need time to learn about a firm's structure and 'culture'. Since workers with specific skills tend to earn more from their firm they are able to negotiate for higher pay, as can be seen in the annual round of bankers' bonuses.

Perhaps the most dramatic example of this phenomenon in action is the marked change in the number of women joining the workforce over the last four decades. Traditionally, women had been far more likely than men to work part-time and inter-mittently, partly because they usually withdrew from the labour market for a while after having children. Social changes, greater working rights for women and the growth in service sector jobs have encouraged more women into the labour market, so providing incentives for investing in higher education. The pay gap between the genders – while still unconscionably large – has declined over time as women bypass traditional 'women's jobs' to enter accounting, law, medicine, engineering and other areas that pay well.

Becker's research opened people's eyes to ways of looking at the labour market. This concept of human capital clearly has tremendous implications for why the distribution of income is skewed in the way that it is (so that there is inequality within the workforce), the distribution of incomes between different age groups, and the patterns of unemployment among unskilled compared with skilled people. More recently his ideas have fed into a new way of looking at growth that properly accounts for human capital – what Nobel laureate Robert Lucas called 'endogenous' growth.

# New home economics

One of Becker's radical pieces of research was to apply an economic interpretation of decision making to how families made decisions. We saw (in Chapter 8) how Paul Samuelson said that families should be seen as units where members cooperate to maximise their overall utility. Becker went further, looking at the allocation of time within the family and using economics to explain why people have children and educate them and why men and women marry and divorce.

His work on human capital had led Becker to thinking about why different children had different opportunities and life patterns. Some children go on to university; some don't. Among those who drop out even earlier, some find their own career path and are very successful – but not all. He was convinced that it was something within the family that could explain the difference. He believed that there were factors at play within each family that resulted from choices its members had taken that in turn influenced the decisions that the children ultimately took for themselves.

> *A household could be regarded as a 'small factory'.*

His answer, which was summarised in his book, *A Treatise on the Family*, was even more provocative than his thinking on human capital and discrimination – even the Nobel award committee called it a 'radical extension of the applicability of economic theory'. His basic idea was that a household could be regarded as a 'small factory' that produces what he called basic goods, such as meals, a home environment, entertainment and so on, using time and input of goods and services that 'the household purchases on the open market'.

He saw that the cost of producing those basic goods is not just the shopping bill but also the time taken (in cooking, cleaning, tidying, organising, etc.). Clearly if the wage of one member of the family changes that will affect how much time they will wish to devote to producing basic goods. This is the implicit economic rationale for why time-poor but well-paid bankers and their spouses will choose to pay home help workers and au pairs to carry out the tasks they might have done when they were less well-off.

But money is not the only issue that people care about when they decide to get married and subsequently allocate household tasks. People will also value love, affection, the other's good looks and wit, and their educational level to gauge some idea of compatibility. However many other facets one could include, Becker still said that people were looking out for their interest, made comparisons between the benefits and the costs of their interests, and chose the life partners they believed would maximise their well-being.

If people are receptacles of human capital, then children must be either consumer durable goods or capital goods, requiring resources of time (childcare) and inputs (food and nappies), but delivering services over time of both a monetary (shares of wages and care in old age) and an intangible (love and affection) nature. The decision to have children must therefore also be an economic investment decision in the same way that Becker saw the choice to marry.

On this analysis couples choose whether and how many

children to have based on a measure of the costs of benefits of having children and they rank those relative to other goods and services. The 'price' of children will vary according to each couple's own choices, their income and the inputs they plan to buy (private versus state education, for example). Given that raising children is an extremely time-intensive activity, especially in the early years, the parents' – and particularly the mother's – price of time will be a crucial ingredient in the decision.

Looked at through this lens, the price of an extra child is much higher for wealthier parents than for poorer ones (the idea of opportunity cost again comes in here). It is noticeable that families in advanced economies have tended to become smaller as women's earnings have risen. People in advanced societies are likely to want to have what Becker called 'higher quality' children – i.e. better educated and skilled rather than morally better – while developing economies might prefer a greater quantity of children who can help with food production in due course. As wages rise, parents increase their investments in human capital, combined with a decrease in the number of children.

Becker also used this analysis to explain rising divorce rates. As women's wages rose this was likely to increase their propensity to divorce. In the past a woman who only had part-time and/or intermittent work would be scared that divorce would have a major impact on her well-being and future quality of life. But if she has a good job and the marriage is deteriorating then she knows she will continue to earn a good income and will not be completely dependent on her husband.

One of Becker's famous ideas is known as the 'rotten kid theorem'. This says that members of a family will act to increase the happiness of all the others, however selfish they are, if they are given the right incentive. Becker used the idea of a wealthy altruistic household head who gives money to his or her offspring. Even a child who takes pleasure from hurting a sibling can be encouraged to change their behaviour by the knowledge they will be rewarded. As a result both altruistic parents and their perhaps selfish children will work out efficient relations within the family.

It is hardly surprising that taken together these ideas would appear distasteful to some. In 1995 the American feminist economist Barbara Bergmann called Becker's findings 'preposterous conclusions',[1] adding: 'Becker's method of thinking about the family leads, as does almost all neoclassical theory, to a conclusion that the institutions depicted are benign, and that government intervention would be useless at best and probably harmful.' Fellow feminist economist Nancy Folbre criticised Becker for justifying a sexual division of labour along traditional homemaker/breadwinner lines by assuming increasing returns to investment in homemaking skills (as a class) and development of skills more commonly required in paid work (as a class).[2] Becker himself acknowledged the criticisms but did not alter his views. Indeed he has pointed out that his second wife, Guity Nashat, who is an Iranian writer on women's issues, agrees with his take on the issue. His writing has provided the bedrock for analysis by many subsequent economists, including Daniel Kahneman, whom we shall meet in the next chapter.

1. Barbara Bergmann, 'Becker's Theory of the Family: preposterous conclusions', *Challenge*, Vol. 39(1) (January–February 1996).
2. Nancy Folbre and Julie Wilson, 'For Love or Money – or Both?', *The Journal of Economic Perspectives*, Vol. 14(4) (Autumn 2000), pp. 123–40.

# Crime and punishment

Becker's inspiration for his major research into the economics of crime and punishment arose from his own misdemeanour. As he recalled in his Nobel lecture, he once found himself running late for an oral examination of a student in economic theory at Columbia University. He had to decide quickly whether to put the car in a parking garage or risk getting a ticket for parking illegally on the street. He calculated the likelihood of getting a ticket, the size of the penalty, and the cost and hassle of putting the car in a lot, decided to take the risk and park on the street and did not get a ticket.

He realised that the parking authorities had probably gone through a similar analysis and based the number of inspections and the size of the penalty on their estimates of how motorists would behave. At the time much of the debate over criminal behaviour was that it was driven by mental illness or was the result of poverty or social oppression. In his innovative style, Becker applied the theories of rational behaviour and human capital to criminal behaviour.

---

*Becker assumed that criminal behaviour was a rational decision.*

---

In other words he assumed that criminal behaviour was a rational decision – the issue was to work out the calculations that went into it. As with marriage, that rationality was not just about monetary gain; some people would include a cost for damage to their own high moral standards in committing a crime. If those standards were very high that person would probably not commit any crime, however minor, and however small the chances of detection and the size of the penalty.

But the size of prison populations implies that there are plenty of other people who do the maths differently. Becker said they would rate the financial rewards from crime compared to lawful work, taking account of the likelihood of apprehension and conviction, and the severity of the punishment. This was the calculus Becker admits he followed at Columbia University. In his book *Crime and Punishment*, Becker said that crime was a full-time or part-time career similar to carpentry, engineering or teaching. It is therefore the difference in anticipated costs and benefits that comes into play rather than pure preferences.

If that is the case then criminals are likely to respond to changes in the 'price' of crime, or, as economists say, the elasticity of the price (the price is elastic where changes lead to marked shifts in demand). This in turn helps the authorities to think about how to deter crime. In other words increasing the penalty will reduce the net benefit to criminals and so reduce the number choosing that career. As Becker himself said, 'punishment works'.[3]

But he also calculated the loss to society, which he said was the sum of the damage to society from the offences, the total costs of catching and convicting the culprits and the cost of imprisonment. On that basis using fines would lower the social cost as it would not require costly prison space and the money could be used to compensate victims. The optimal fine in his view was one that just offset both the harm to the victim and the legal costs of processing the criminal through the legal system.

---

3. Gary Becker, 'Economics Analysis and Human Behaviour', in J. Green and J.H. Kagel (eds), *Advances in Behavioural Economics*, Vol. 1 (Ablex Publishing Corp., 1987).

By looking at the probability of conviction and the severity of the punishment (in terms of either money or time or freedom lost) Becker was able to examine the impact of any punishment system and how it related to different income groups. For example, he said that Class A Misdemeanours (for example, burglary or ABH) in 1965 carried a year-long jail term or a fine of no more than $1,000. Becker believed this put too high a price on the jail term relative to the fine. While a wealthy person would readily pay $1,000 to avoid losing their liberty for a year, a poor convict would have no choice and would have to accept the jail term – however long it was. This was therefore unfair to poor offenders, who could not pay the fine and so had to face jail.

It was not that Becker necessarily had a view about which fine or jail term should be raised or lowered. It was more that he realised that by looking at the 'prices' of the penalties one could see the market consequences for different people. As he said in his essay on the issue: 'Since economics has been developed to handle resource allocation, an "economic" framework becomes applicable to, and helps enrich the analysis of criminal behaviour.'[4]

One option to reduce the social cost of crime would therefore be to increase penalties to take advantage of the deterrent effect while reducing the amount spent on enforcement, as there would be less need for apprehension and conviction thanks to a lower crime rate. On the other hand, Becker suggested increasing enforcement of more costly crimes, which would probably mean increasing enforcement in wealthy areas and decreasing it in poor areas.

---

4. Gary Becker, 'Crime and Punishment: an economic approach', *Journal of Political Economy*, Vol. 76(2) (March–April 1968), pp. 169–217.

His thinking on human capital indicated that the authorities could also reduce crime by improving the lawful employment options – jobs that could be secured by those who otherwise would be likely to go into crime. As major violent crimes were typically committed by people from poorer backgrounds and low income opportunities, it would make economic sense to improve their employment chances.


# Drug addiction ... and human behaviour

Perhaps the most adventurous of Becker's applications of the doctrine of rational behaviour to the human sphere of life was in the issue of drug addiction. Together with fellow Chicagoan Kevin Murphy, he put together a theory of rational addiction that saw addicts as people seeking to maximise their utility over time. They looked at addiction as a whole, whether to work, exercise, or religion as well as to drugs, alcohol or tobacco.

While acknowledging the physiological powers of some habit-forming activities, they said that addicts know very well how the activity will affect them and so the reason they consume more and more is that this is the pattern of consumption that makes them happiest. Each time they take crack/smoke a cigarette/drink wine/go to the gym, they have weighed up the costs and benefits. For example, a smoker will value the benefits of one more cigarette against the costs of buying that cigarette, including both the actual price, the health damages from the cigarette, and the costs of increased future smoking resulting from greater addiction. Addicts tend to discount those future costs heavily.

Increasing the cost of addictive goods – by taxing legal goods and raising the penalties for using illegal ones – would have some beneficial impacts in reducing addicts' use. Becker and Murphy said that over the long term demand for addictive goods was more elastic – responded more to the price – than that for non-addictive goods. But they said the best way to end the addiction was by going 'cold turkey', which was also a rational response. The decision is rational because addicts can see that they are exchanging extreme but short-term pain for large long-term gains of being addiction-free.

The theory has been criticised for treating a problem that involves complex health, neurological and physiological issues with economics. Economist Ole Rogeberg has used it as a case example of what he calls 'absurd theories' in economics. He says that it 'illustrate[s] how absurd choice theories in economics get taken seriously as possibly true explanations and tools for welfare analysis despite being poorly interpreted, empirically unfalsifiable, and based on wildly inaccurate assumptions selectively justified by ad hoc stories'.[5]

One criticism is that it does seem absurd to say that addicts are acting rationally when so many are clearly unhappy. Becker and Murphy acknowledged that addicts were often unhappy people but said that did not undermine their arguments that it was rational. They said that many people became addicts as a result of some major personal trauma, such as divorce or a death, which had reduced their quality of life. The addiction was a response to that but also a way of maximising their utility within that situation.

---

5. Ole Rogeberg, 'Taking Absurd Theories Seriously: economics and the case of rational addiction theories', *Philosophy of Science*, Vol. 71 (2004), pp. 263–85.

However, other studies have backed up the theory. A study by Becker and Murphy together with American health economist Michael Grossman provided empirical evidence that higher prices tomorrow will lead to lower consumption today.[6] According to a survey of a large number of papers, these findings have been used as the standard approach to modelling consumption of goods such as cigarettes,[7] and have been backed up by some but not all empirical evidence.

# Long-term impact

Gary Becker revolutionised the way that people thought about human behaviour. What many of the specific theories mentioned above have in common is that they are the result of using an economics analysis of rational people's assessments of the costs and benefits of any particular activity, whether going to college, committing a crime, getting married or having another drink. Becker saw that people consistently sought to maximise their utility using a stable set of personal preferences and as much information as they could acquire.

Becker effectively took the microeconomic ideas set out by Adam Smith and others and brought them into the context of the 20th century. He developed an approach that was applicable to all human behaviour, not just the sale and purchase

---

6. G. Becker, M. Grossman and K.M. Murphy, 'An Empirical Analysis of Cigarette Addiction', *American Economic Review*, Vol. LXXXIV (1994), pp. 396–418.

7. J. Gruber and H. Koszegi, 'Is Addiction Rational? Theory and evidence', *The Quarterly Journal of Economics* (November 2001), pp. 1261–1304.

of goods and services. It was something that could be applied to all decisions both large and small, to repeated or one-off decisions, for emotional and mechanical ends, as well as by patients and doctors, business people or politicians, or by teachers and students as well as by families.

The specific theories that Becker produced still have echoes in many areas of public policy today. The idea that discrimination is costly to the discriminator is both common sense among economists today, and part of the reason why governments insist that employers and service providers cannot discriminate on the basis of prejudice.

It has also fuelled future research. Nobel laureates Edmund Phelps and Kenneth Arrow built on Becker's work to show that the beliefs held by employers, teachers and other influential groups that minority members are less productive can be self-fulfilling, for these beliefs may cause minorities to under-invest in their education, training and work skills and this under-investment does make them less productive.

While Becker did not invent the term human capital, it is his economic rationalisation of the idea that has led to the term being widely used and understood by policymakers, employers and business consultants today. The idea of improving the overall performance of the economy as well as the earnings-potential of individuals is now a centrepiece of many official economic development programmes. Governments offer tax incentives aimed at encouraging workers and employers to invest in education or on-the-job training.

It is no exaggeration to say that the discipline of the economics of the family is Gary Becker's creation. Issues such as marriage, fertility, family planning and division of labour within the household were not given any proper economic analysis until Becker and colleagues undertook the research. The foundational assumptions of the economic approach – maximising behaviour and equilibrium – are now widely accepted not only by economists but also by family sociologists, demographers and others who study the family.

---

*The discipline of the economics of the family is Gary Becker's creation.*

---

By establishing the idea that all decisions can be explained as a rational assessment of costs and benefits, Becker opened the door to a host of tax changes and legal reforms aimed at influencing the way that people behave, whether it is to have fewer children, smoke fewer cigarettes or to invest in a work-related training scheme. The same analytic techniques can be used to improve the enforcement of laws ranging from minimum wage limits, clean air legislation, rules on insider trader and income tax evasions.

As Becker himself said in his Nobel lecture, it was already clear that many economists wanted to work on social issues rather than issues forming the traditional core of economics. 'At the same time, specialists from fields that do consider social questions are often attracted to the economic way of modelling behaviour because of the analytical power provided by the assumption of individual rationality,' he said.

'Thriving schools of rational choice theorists and empirical researchers are active in sociology, law, political science, history, anthropology, and psychology. The rational choice model provides the most promising basis presently available for a unified approach to the analysis of the social world by scholars from the social sciences.'

Late on in life Becker has still been influencing the debate. He wrote a monthly column for the magazine *Business Week* from 1985 to 2004, alternating with liberal Princeton economist Alan Blinder. He established a widely read blog with Judge Richard Posner, the Becker–Posner Blog,[8] and as recently as December 2013 was writing about how proposals to raise the minimum wage in the US would harm young vulnerable people struggling to find work. Earlier that year he hit the headlines when he called for drugs to be decriminalised as the best way to bring down addiction rates and end the violence associated with the drugs trade.[9] It is clear he is determined not to enjoy a quiet retirement.

# Verdict: credits and debits

Gary Becker has earned his place in the pantheon of great economists with his reformulation of the theory of consumer behaviour. As a result policymakers and experts in other fields now see that economic thinking can add a whole new dimension to problem solving. Using the assumptions of stable preferences, maximising behaviour, market equilibrium and rational choice, economists can offer new insights into what is not traditionally seen as their purview – just as Adam Smith did in the late 18th century.

---

8. http://uchicagolaw.typepad.com/beckerposner/
9. Gary Becker and Kevin Murphy, 'Have We Lost the War on Drugs?', *Wall Street Journal*, 4 January 2013.

However, Becker has been criticised by both economists
– for introducing too broad a set of values – and by non-econo-
mists – for applying rational monetary analysis to emotional
decisions. In the wake of the global financial crisis, where
assumptions about rational human behaviour appeared to
contribute to the disaster, the pendulum of opinion has swung
towards the latter critics.

# Further reading

Gary Becker, *Economics of Discrimination*, 2nd edn (University
of Chicago Press, 1971).

Gary Becker, *Human Capital*, 3rd edn (University of Chicago
Press, 2009).

Gary Becker, *A Treatise on the Family*, 2nd edn (Harvard
University Press, 1983).

Ramón Febrero and Pedro S. Schwartz (eds), *The Essence of
Becker*, Hoover Institution (1995).

Robert Pollak, 'Gary Becker's Contributions to Family and
Household Economics', NBER Working Paper (2002).

# CHAPTER 10

# Daniel Kahneman – economic psychologist

'Economists think about what people ought to do.
Psychologists watch what they actually do.'
*Daniel Kahneman, Interview with CNN Money,*
*23 August 2007*

I must state one important thing before going any further: Daniel Kahneman is a psychologist. So why is he included in a book on ten great economists when there are so many professionally trained economists to choose from? On one level the answer is easy. Kahneman won the Nobel Prize for economic sciences in 2002 jointly with Vernon Smith, an experimental economist (Kahneman's collaborator, Amos Tversky, died in 1996, so making him ineligible for the Nobel). Kahneman's citation was for 'integrating insights from psychological research into economic science, especially concerning human judgment and decision-making under uncertainty – thereby laying the foundation for a new field of research'.

But from a broader perspective Kahneman is the prime example of a growing trend towards taking a multidisciplinary approach to economic problems, drawing on maths, computer science, biology, evolutionary science, geology and psychology as well the core areas of economics and finance. The idea of a *homo economicus* – or economic human – motivated by self-interest and capable of rational decision-making is now increasingly seen as a model that fails to explain how the economy operates in practice. People can behave in ways that appear irrational, and a failure to acknowledge that is likely to lead to a misinterpretation of how the economy works.

Daniel Kahneman is a key mover behind the discipline of behavioural economics, which is a fast-growing and fascinating field that has become of increasing importance for governments and businesses as well as for economic policymakers and academics. It seeks to improve our understanding of how people make economic and financial choices and decisions. By blending economic analysis with techniques from psychology we can gain a better understanding of how people make important economic decisions that affect both their own well-being and that of the economy as a whole.

# Early life and influences

Daniel Kahneman was born in Tel Aviv, in what is now Israel, in 1934 while his mother was visiting her extended family in British Mandatory Palestine. His parents had emigrated from Lithuania and settled in Paris, where Daniel was brought up during the Nazi occupation of France. It was one event during this traumatic era that appears to have provided his inspiration to investigate human behaviour.

Kahneman has often cited the story of how one night he overstayed a visit to a Christian friend and so had to walk home illegally in the dark. He had turned inside out the jumper with the yellow star that the Nazis had ordered all Jews to wear and was trying to be inconspicuous. However, on the deserted street he was spotted by an SS soldier, who summoned him over. But rather than examine or interrogate him the soldier picked him up, hugged him, showed him a photograph of his son and gave him some money. Kahneman later said this had a 'big impact' on his life. 'I went home more certain than ever that my mother was right: people were endlessly complicated and interesting.'

The family, minus his father, who had succumbed to tuberculosis in 1944, emigrated to Palestine, where Kahneman thrived academically. When he went for vocational guidance, psychology emerged as the top recommendation, with economics not too far behind. After the creation of the state of Israel, and with a psychology degree in his pocket, when time came to do national service he was assigned to the psychology branch of the Israel Defense Force.

One of his tasks was to run an assessment for an officer training scheme that had originally been designed by the British Army. It involved assembling a team of soldiers, known only by their numbers, who had to lift a telephone pole over a 2.5-metre high wall without allowing it to touch the ground or the wall. Kahneman and his colleagues gave the candidates marks but subsequently found their grading had little link with the performance of the candidates in later training. Despite knowing the test to be virtually worthless, they continued to carry out the tests and write up the results. Kahneman described this as the 'illusion of validity', which he would expand on later.

Kahneman developed his academic career, gaining a PhD at the University of California at Berkeley, before returning to Israel where he became a lecturer at the Hebrew University in Jerusalem. It was there that he met Amos Tversky, who was to become his key collaborator. Indeed, Kahneman himself said that his Nobel was awarded for work that they produced during that period of 'intense collaboration'. They worked almost exclusively as a duo for more than a decade, during which Kahneman produced some of his most influential work on economics and finance. He is currently professor of psychology emeritus at Princeton University and professor of psychology and public affairs emeritus at Princeton's Woodrow Wilson School of Public and International Affairs. As well as economics Kahneman has written on cognitive psychology, judgement and happiness.

# Economic writings and theories

At the heart of Kahneman's contribution to economics is his analysis of how people make decisions and particularly financial decisions. Given that an integral part of economics is the collective weight of the decisions that millions of people and businesses make every day, it is important to understand how each one makes those decisions especially in the face of uncertain outcomes. The first step in this analysis is to accept that people often appear not to behave rationally.

---

*People often appear not to behave rationally.*

---

There is a division within rationality: between what people understand to be rational behaviour and how they in fact act. In other words there is a gap between how people think they should behave, and how they do behave in real life (what both economists and psychologists call normative and positive). It became increasingly obvious to psychologists such as Kahneman that traditional models of rational decision-making, which make assumptions about people's behaviour, do not fully reflect human nature. For instance, it is unclear why *homo economicus* would help a friend, care for other people or donate money to charity.

One of Kahneman and Tversky's first insights was that people made decisions either by intuition or by deliberate reasoning, which they called System 1 and System 2 respectively. Kahneman described these intuitive decisions as being fast, automatic and effortless, generating impressions of what was going on. In other words, people took mental short cuts even when making extremely large and important financial decisions. Reasoned judgements were taken more slowly and in a serial, effortful and deliberately controlled fashion. Kahneman set out this idea for a wider audience in his book *Thinking, Fast and Slow*.

In his Nobel lecture Kahneman gave a clever example of what he meant. He used a question given to economics students: 'A bat and a ball cost $1.10 in total. The bat costs $1 more than the ball. How much does the ball cost?' He said that more than half the students at Princeton and Michigan universities gave the answer 10 cents, probably because the total sum neatly divides into $1 and 10 cents (although in that case the total would be $1.20). Only after a bit of careful thinking do you see that the answer is 5 cents – the difference between a bat costing $1.05 and a ball costing 5 cents is $1 and the total is $1.10. This highlights the difference between the two systems of thinking.

### Heuristics and bias

If people tend to make many decisions on an intuitive basis it is critical to understand what the thought processes are that guide so-called rational people to make decisions that might appear in the cold light of day to be irrational. Kahneman focused on the mental short cuts that people use when faced with uncertain and often complex decisions and which psychologists call heuristics (from the ancient Greek meaning to find out or discover), or what we might call rules of thumb. While these work a lot of the time and are tools people find useful, they involve making mental connections that are not logical and can lead to severe and systematic errors. Kahneman and Tversky called the errors that follow 'cognitive biases'.

In their 1974 paper[1] Kahneman and Tversky identified three heuristics:

- *Availability*, where someone assesses the probability of an event by the ease with which other occurrences can be brought to mind. For instance, a middle-aged person who has friends who have suffered heart attacks will attach a relatively higher risk to that than other more statistically important threats.

- *Representativeness*, where people look to see whether two events resemble each other to help them to decide whether there is a connection between the two. For example, when hearing someone described as bookish, shy and retiring and asked whether they are more likely to be a librarian or a shop worker, many people will choose librarian. While this seems instinctively right (using System 1), it is only when one remembers (using System 2) that there are many times more shop workers than librarians in the working population that one realises that the odds of anyone being a librarian are tiny.

- *Anchoring and adjustment*, where different starting points or references lead to different estimates. For instance, workers negotiating a pay rise will probably start bargaining against the first offer made by their employer rather than their goal.

Each of these heuristics led to a range of biases that emerged from the misapplication of these decision-making short cuts. Kahneman identified six biases that emerged from the representativeness heuristic: *base-rate neglect*; *insensitivity to*

---

1. Amos Tversky and Daniel Kahneman, 'Judgment under Uncertainty: heuristics and biases', *Science*, New Series, Vol. 185(4157) (27 September 1974), pp. 1124–1131.

*sample size*; *misconceptions of chance*; *insensitivity to predicta-bility*; *the illusion of validity*; and *misconceptions of regression*. What these complex-sounding phenomena have in common is that people use similarities or associations rather than logical deduction to come to a conclusion.

There is not space to detail all six, but two examples show how susceptible we are to error. The *insensitivity to predict-ability* means that people are confident about making decisions based on insufficient evidence. Two groups of students were asked to give their views after attending a lecture given by a student teacher: one on the lesson and the other on his expected career performance in five years' time. Both groups gave very similar assessments even though one lesson is an unlikely predictor of medium-term career success. This may explain why investors often go with a stockbroker or an entre-preneur based on one recent success. The *illusion of validity*, which Kahneman first identified in the Israeli army officer tests, describes the way people use evidence they know to be irrelevant to justify their decisions.

The *misconception of chance* is also known as the *gambler's fallacy*. In a famous example, gamblers at the Monte Carlo Casino in 1913 are said to have lost millions of francs by betting heavily that a streak of consecutive black numbers on a roulette wheel would be followed by a run of reds. In fact, black came up 15 consecutive times, leading to substantial losses for the players who had kept betting frantically on red at earlier turns of the wheel. The idea that a repeated pattern, such as a roulette wheel coming up black, must at some point be reversed is very common – even though the wheel of course has no memory of the past. The same bias can explain why investors buy into falling share prices on the expectation that at some point at least they must rise.

The availability heuristic in turn leads to biases, including the *retrievability, imaginability* and *illusory correlation biases.* Events that are easy to recall or which readily spring to mind – and so can easily be 'retrieved' – are more likely to be used by someone making a quick decision than information that would have to be researched. Similarly, events that can be imagined – such as the possible risks involved in taking an airplane – will be given greater weight than ones that are harder to conceive. Thus a bomb on board a plane – a thankfully rare event – may seem a greater risk than the failure of a microprocessor in an engine or human error.

Biases emerging from the anchoring heuristic include the insufficient adjustment bias that results from people's inability to abandon their first impressions when new information arrives late in the process. Kahneman and Tversky highlighted the ease with which it is possible to 'anchor' people's thinking by asking them to estimate the percentage of African countries in the United Nations. The researchers spun a wheel of fortune with numbers between 0 and 100. The subjects were told to estimate the proportion of African nations by moving upward or downward from the given number. The arbitrary numbers produced by the wheel had a marked effect on estimates. For example, the median estimates of the percentage of African countries in the UN were 25 per cent and 45 per cent for groups that received 10 and 65, respectively, as starting points (the true answer is 28 per cent).

## From psychology to economics

We can already see how these biases and errors in thinking affect the way that people make financial decisions. When a large number of people and businesses are making these mistakes there is clearly the potential for these to impact on the wider economy and on financial stability. The list of biases is long and growing. But there are some that have particularly affected the way that economists have looked at how people take financial decisions, which we will look at in more detail.

---

*Biases and errors in thinking affect the way that people make financial decisions.*

---

One is the *optimism bias*. In terms of its consequences for decisions, the optimistic bias may well be the most significant cognitive bias. This exploits the fact that most of us view the world as more benign than it really is, our own skills as more valuable than they truly are, and the targets we set as more achievable than they are likely to be. We also tend to exaggerate our ability to forecast the future, which in turn fosters overconfidence.

Kahneman says that this bias is more predominant among successful and influential people such as business people, traders and politicians. On top of that, following the *optimism bias* tends to lead people or institutions voluntarily to take on significant risks. They are likely to underestimate the risks of failure, and overestimate the likelihood of their strategy working and the rewards that will flow from it. In good times that can be no bad thing, as it means they are more likely to benefit from confident decisions.

But, as Kahneman explains in *Thinking, Fast and Slow*, leaders of large businesses sometimes make huge bets in high-value mergers and acquisitions, acting on the mistaken belief that they can manage the assets of another company better than its current owners do. Stock market investors usually respond by downgrading the value of the acquiring firm, because experience has shown that such efforts fail more often than they succeed. Misguided acquisitions have been explained by a 'hubris hypothesis': the executives of the acquiring firm are simply less competent than they think they are.

This overconfidence can be seen as a contributor to the global financial crisis as traders took out huge risky transactions, backing their own ability. The impact of this overconfidence was probably reinforced by another bias. Kahneman has cited a study of chief financial officers carried out by Duke University in the US showing that there was no correlation between their forecasts for the stock market and what actually happened.

There are many more biases that show that people make decisions in a way that reveals that people's preferences are not stable, as classical economists say, but can shift according to how they understand the choice open to them (i.e. because they have reframed it). These include:

- *Hindsight bias*, which encourages people to infer their own skills from successes that were down to luck or timing. A stockbroker who rode a share price boom will believe he is a genius, which in turn fuels his optimism bias.

- *Confirmation bias*, or the tendency to place more emphasis on evidence that favours your existing view and ignore that which does not. An investor with a negative view of a company will tend to read and remember negative news and brush over positive developments.

- *Status quo bias* – a preference to stick with what we know, which means we discount the value of alternatives even if we are assured they are much better. This can help explain the relatively small number of people who switch banks or energy providers despite evidence that there are cheaper alternatives.

## *Prospect Theory*

Prospect Theory is at the heart of Kahneman's Nobel Prize and one of the many that he developed with Tversky. It refers to the idea of a gamble and the gambler's 'prospect' of winning or losing in the face of risk and uncertainty. In fact it later emerged that the authors only picked the name 'Prospect Theory' to ensure it stuck in people's minds.[2] Until they came along, economists dealt with decisions made in the face of uncertainty through something called the expected utility theory (EUT). This said that people made decisions by working out their utility by multiplying the gain by the probability of winning.

However, Kahneman and Tversky ran a number of experiments with volunteers that gave people two sets of options to choose from. They published the results in 1979 in *Prospect Theory: an analysis of decisions under risk*, the most cited paper ever to appear in *Econometrica*, the prestigious academic journal of economics.[3] The results showed that people were not consistent in applying the same methodology to the alternatives. In one particular set, they offered these choices:

Prospect A: a 33% chance of winning $2,500; a 66% chance of $2,400; and a 1% chance of zero
versus
Prospect B: a certain win of $2,400

---

2. https://chronicle.com/article/The-Anatomy-of-Influence/129688/
3. Daniel Kahneman and Amos Tversky, *Econometrica*, Vol. 47(2) (March 1979), pp. 263–92.

and

Prospect C: a 33% chance of $2,500; and a 67% chance of zero
versus
Prospect D: a 34% chance of $2,400; and a 66% chance of zero

Someone who picks A is a risk-seeker and according to the EUT should then also pick C as both have longer odds for a higher win. Risk-averse people should pick the safer options of B and D. In fact 18% picked A, but 83% chose C (and so 82% picked B but only 17% picked D). They repeated these experiments time and again using different combinations but the results showed people consistently avoided being consistent with the EUT.

The pair said this showed that people put different weights on certain outcomes and behaved very differently when offered a guaranteed outcome to when they were offered one that is slightly less likely (but still probable). They called this the *certainty effect*. When they offered people choices between two outcomes that were identical – except that one set involved a loss and the other a gain (i.e. an 80% chance of a $4,000 loss or a certain loss of $3,000; and then an 80% chance of a $4,000 gain or a certain gain of $3,000), the vast majority of people (80:20) chose the certain gain over the chance of a higher win, but 92% preferred to take the 20% of losing $4,000 and just 8% preferred the guaranteed loss of $3,000. The EUT would say they would choose the matching pair. This idea that people would make totally different choices between options that mirrored each other is called the *reflection effect*.

According to Kahneman, the EUT idea, which was first set out by the Swiss scientist Daniel Bernoulli in 1738 and so had held sway for some 250 years, was flawed in two key ways:

- People's views of good or bad bets are based on the change in their wealth as a result, not just its level. If two people owned £5 million today but yesterday Jack had £1 million and Jill £9 million, EUT would say that Jill and Jack would be equally happy today while common sense would indicate she would be despondent while Jack would be elated.

- People assess whether they will make a loss or gain relative to a reference point. Now let's say that Jack has £1 million and Jill £4 million. Both are offered a 50:50 chance to end up with £1 million or £4 million or end up with £2 million for sure. EUT would expect them both to choose the gamble as that way they can both expect to be left with £2.5 million from the gamble (the average outcome of the £1 million and £4 million bet) or a guaranteed £2 million. But in real life Jack will go for the sure-fire option that doubles his money while Jill, who faces a loss if she takes the £2 million, will take the bet for at least a chance of retaining her £4 million. What counts is their current state of wealth.

Kahneman and Tversky argued that people made choices as the result of a two-stage process. First they frame the choices as gains or losses relative to a reference point, which may often be the gambler's current wealth rather than zero. The second stage is to evaluate the prospects to identify the one with the greatest value. This involves both an assessment of the mathematical probabilities but also a subjective view of the outcomes, particularly set against the reference point.

They found that people were more worried about suffering a loss then they were about making a gain, that they valued a sure gain over a probable gain (the certainty effect) and that they preferred a probable loss over a certain loss. Adam Smith had alluded to this idea of loss aversion when he said, 'we suffer more ... when we fall from a better to a worse situation than we ever enjoy when we rise from a worse to a better'.[4] Kahneman said that people were driven more strongly to avoid losses than to achieve gains. A reference point is sometimes the status quo, but it can also be a goal in the future: not achieving a goal is a loss; exceeding it is a gain.

---

*People were more worried about suffering a loss then they were about making a gain.*

---

The problems occur when one party wants to avoid losses and another to make gains. Good examples in real life are renegotiations of existing contracts such as pay agreements between managers and unions or global trade agreements between large and small countries. Loss aversion creates an asymmetry that makes agreements hard to reach, Kahneman says.

Loss aversion affects how people behave on the high street, in the workplace and at home. Kahneman and colleagues found that in this situation the existing sale price, wage or rent sets the reference point, which creates a position that must not be infringed. People see that companies are behaving unfairly if they try to impose losses (relative to the reference point) by hiking prices or rents or trimming wages – unless they can show that it is to defend their own position. Shops that double the price of umbrellas ahead of torrential rain are seen as sharks – even though their action fits firmly within rational economics.

---

4. Adam Smith, *The Theory of Moral Sentiments* (1759), Part VI, Sect. 1.

The significance is that assumptions of rational behaviour that simply look at the chances of a particular gamble coming off without any reference to the financial position of the gambler ignore the impact that the phrasing of the bet can have, and the way that people's aversion to suffering losses can alter the way they make decisions.

The danger of loss aversion is that it leads us to try to minimise these feelings of loss – even when it does not make financial sense to do so. Loss aversion has a noticeable effect in the housing market as evidence suggests that people are often unwilling to sell their home for less than they paid for it. Their reference point is what they paid for it in the past rather than its current value, which may be about to fall further.

This problem is compounded by the *endowment effect*, a bias that makes people give a higher value to something that they now own compared with before they acquired it. In other words they value things more simply because they own them. The endowment effect, a term coined by Kahneman's collaborator Richard Thaler, is the difference between what people are willing to accept (WTA) for something they own and the price they are willing to pay (WTP) for something they do not yet have. Thaler had seen that an economics professor who was a wine collector would never pay more than $35 for a bottle but never sell for less than $100, even though EUT would say he was sacrificing up to $65 profit each time he held on to the bottle. The endowment effect built on prospect theory by saying that someone who owns something is valuing the pain (loss) of giving up ownership while a buyer is measuring the pleasure of getting hold of the good.

# Long-term legacy

The research carried out by Kahneman with various partners, and especially with Tversky, clearly challenged the traditional model of rational choice that had underpinned thinking since Adam Smith. By carrying out copious and repeated experiments using real people making decisions in laboratory environments, he was able to show how these heuristics and biases revealed fundamental weaknesses in the rational theory and explained how people really make decisions. By doing this he was able, as his Nobel citation said, to lay the foundation for a new field of research.

Kahneman can therefore be seen as the father of behavioural economics, which is now seen as a field in its own right. Many of those who worked with him, studied under him, or were simply inspired by him, have built on his findings to further refine the genre. Policymakers increasingly accept the findings of the research by Kahneman and others into behavioural economics and finance.

In the UK, the Cabinet Office has established a Behavioural Insights Team while the Department for Food and Rural Affairs has set up a Centre of Expertise on Influencing Behaviour. Regulatory bodies across the world such as the US Federal Trade Commission, the UK Office for Fair Trading, the OECD and the Australian Productivity Commission have begun to take behavioural economics into serious consideration and have already carried out behavioural studies to inform some of their regulatory policies. The EU's competition authority used behavioural economics in the recent Microsoft competition case when it insisted that its products offered a selection of rival internet browsers as well as Microsoft's own Explorer.

We have seen how Thaler coined the term *endowment effect* to capture and expand on Kahneman's finding that people value things more highly once they own them. Thaler, who is a professor of behavioural science and economics at Chicago University, built on the Prospect Theory to devise a positive theory of consumer choice – how people actually make decisions compared with how they should. He coined the phrase *choice architecture* with law professor Cass Sunstein to describe the way in which decisions may (and can) be influenced by how the choices are presented.

Thaler has developed many strands of thinking in behavioural economics, encapsulated in his book written with Sunstein aimed at a mass market, *Nudge: improving decisions about health, wealth and happiness*, which makes use of Kahneman's three heuristics. This book particularly focuses on how policymakers can use behavioural economics to adapt laws to achieve outcomes by using non-coercive policies to encourage people to save more and become smarter investors. Perhaps the most famous example is the recommendation to change the default option on employment contracts so that a new worker automatically joins the pension scheme unless they opt out (rather than the other way round).

Dan Ariely also hit the best-sellers chart with his book *Predictably Irrational*, while perhaps the best-known title is *Freakonomics* by Chicago economics professor Steve Levitt and journalist Stephen Dubner. Kahneman himself has furthered the popular understanding of behavioural economics through his book, *Thinking, Fast and Slow*, which has won several awards. In 2013 he was awarded the US Presidential Medal of Freedom.

# Verdict: credits and debits

Kahneman's findings have laid the foundations for the rapidly expanding discipline of behavioural economics, which is being increasingly used by financial policymakers such as finance ministries as well as other government departments and in central banks. Kahneman himself has cited the admission in 2008 by former US Federal Reserve chairman Alan Greenspan that he had been wrong in relying on the self-interest of banks to ensure that the financial markets corrected themselves in time as a major event in the development of behavioural economics.[5]

Kahneman acts as the bridge between the first ideas set out 250 years by Adam Smith, who opened this book, and the present day. While Smith is best remembered for the doctrine of enlightened self-interest, it is easy to forget that in his early writings Smith recognised the 'sympathy' that people had for each other and their desire to 'render their happiness'. Kahneman, together with Tversky, Thaler and others, has added many complex layers of understanding what people and businesses are really doing when they think they are making rational decisions.

*Kahneman's work has brought the focus of economics back to the study of individual actors in the economy.*

---

5. Jeremy Clift, 'Questioning a Chastened Priesthood', *Finance & Development*, Vol. 46(3) (International Monetary Fund, September 2009).

Kahneman's work has also brought the focus of economics back to the study of individual actors in the economy and away from the focus on the big picture of macroeconomics that dominated much of the last century. There is little doubt that the whole field of economics has been transformed by the insights of behavioural economists such as Kahneman. But the challenge for his disciples and successors is to show that behavioural economics can provide a catch-all theory for running an economy, rather than just showing where the theories of rational expectations and behaviour fall short.

# What you should take away

- Despite being a psychologist, Kahneman (and Tversky) pretty much created the field of behavioural economics.

- His work has undermined much of the assumptions behind the mainstream acceptance of rational behaviour as the basis for economics.

- His focus on the importance of understanding how people make decisions is increasingly incorporated by governments in financial decision making and regulation

- The creation of a systemic understanding of heuristics and bias has greater improved the ability of policymakers to understand how people make decisions and to help them avoid making bad ones.

- Overconfidence in positive outcomes and in the decision-makers' own abilities contribute to financial booms and busts.

- People often fail to fully account for the risks they are taking.

# Further reading

Dan Ariely, *Predictably Irrational* (HarperCollins, 2009).

Daniel Kahneman, *Attention and Effort* (Prentice-Hall, 1973).

Daniel Kahneman, *Prospect Theory: an analysis of decision under risk* (PN, 1977).

Daniel Kahneman, *Thinking, Fast and Slow* (Penguin, 2012).

Daniel Kahneman, Paul Slovic and Amos Tversky (eds), *Judgment under Uncertainty: heuristics and biases* (Cambridge University Press, 1982).

Richard A. Thaler and Cass R. Sunstein, *Nudge* (Penguin, 2009).

# Index